TRAILBLAZER

EMPOWERING YOUNG MINDS

Common University Entrance Test for Under Graduate Programmes

National Testing Agency (NTA)

CUET (UG)

Section II BUSINESS STUDIES

Author

BINDU BHATIA ARORA

M.Com, B.Ed, PGDM (Sales & Marketing)

Ex. P.G.T. Delhi Public School, Siliguri, West Bengal

Ex. P.G.T. Army Public School, Darjeeling, West Bengal

Ex. P.G.T. Convent of Jesus & Mary, Vadodara, Gujarat

Ex. P.G.T. St. James School, Binnaguri, West Bengal

UNICORN BOOKS

Publishers
UNICORN BOOKS
F-2/16, Ansari Road, Daryaganj, New Delhi-110002
☎ 011-23262683, 23250704
E-mail: info@unicornbooks.in

ISBN 978-81-7806-577-9
Edition: 2023

Printed at : Param Offsetters, Okhla, New Delhi-110020

Introduction

The Common University Entrance Test CUET (UG) is the single entrance test to get admission in the Central Universities and their affiliated colleges for their Undergraduate Programmes. This exam shall be conducted by the National Testing Agency (NTA), which has been established by the Ministry of Education, as an independent, autonomous, self-reliant and self-sustained premier testing organization.

The CUET (UG) will provide a single common platform and equal opportunity to students seeking admission in any of the Central Universities across the country including candidates from the three National Boards, CBSE, AICSE and NIOS.

In the past, candidates had the grievance that though they scored 99% in class XII, they could not get admission in the Universities of their choice. This was basically because of varied typology of questions and scoring pattern across different Boards in the country. These things will get standardized with the introduction CUET (UG).

It is expected that many state universities, deemed to be universities, private universities and other Higher Educational Institutions would be adopting this exam very soon.

Each institution will prepare its Merit List as per its own criteria and admit the candidates based on the NTA CUET score. They may also consider class XII marks.

Candidates who wish to appear for CUET (UG) are advised to go through the required eligibility of the desired University/Universities for selecting the options from UG Programmes being offered.

Examination Structure for CUET (UG)

CUET will basically test conceptual understanding and the ability to apply knowledge, and shall aim to eliminate the need for taking coaching for these exams.

CUET (UG) will consist of the following 4 Sections:

- **Section IA** – 13 Languages
- **Section IB** – 20 Languages
- **Section II** – 27 Domain specific Subjects
- **Section III** – General Test

Choosing options from each Section is not mandatory. Choices should match the requirements of the desired University.

Broad features of CUET (UG) are as follows:

Section	Subjects/ Tests	Questions to be Attempted	Question Type	Duration
Section IA - Languages	There are 13* different languages. Any of these languages may be chosen.	40 questions to be attempted out of 50 in each language	Language to be tested through Reading Comprehension (based on different types of passages– Factual, Literary and Narrative, [Literary Aptitude and Vocabulary]	45 Minutes for each language
Section IB - Languages	There are 20** Languages. Any other language apart from those offered in Section I A may be chosen.			
Section II - Domain	There are 27*** Domains specific subjects being offered under this Section. A candidate may choose a maximum of **Six (06)** Domains as desired by the applicable University/ Universities.	40 Questions to be attempted out of 50	• Input text can be used for MCQ Based Questions • MCQs based on NCERT Class XII syllabus only	45 Minutes for each Domain Specific Subjects.
Section III- General Test	For any such undergraduate programme/ programmes being offered by Universities where a General Test is being used for admission.	60 Questions to be attempted out of 75	• Input text can be used for MCQ Based Questions • General Knowledge, Current Affairs, General Mental Ability, Numerical Ability, Quantitative Reasoning (Simple application of basic mathematical concepts arithmetic/algebra geometry mensuration/s tat taught till Grade 8), Logical and Analytical Reasoning	60 Minutes

*** Languages (13):** Tamil, Telugu, Kannada, Malayalam, Marathi, Gujarati, Odiya, Bengali, Assamese, Punjabi, English, Hindi and Urdu

**** Languages (20):** French, Spanish, German, Nepali, Persian, Italian, Arabic, Sindhi, Sanskrit, Kashmiri, Konkani, Bodo, Dogri, Maithili, Manipuri, Santhali, Tibetan, Japanese, Russian, Chinese.

***** Domain Specific Subjects (27):** 1. Accountancy/Book Keeping; 2. Biology/ Biological Studies/ Biotechnology/Biochemistry; 3. Business Studies; 4. Chemistry; 5. Computer Science/Informatics Practices; 6. Economics/Business Economics; 7. Engineering Graphics; 8. Entrepreneurship; 9. Geography/Geology; 10. History; 11. Home Science; 12. Knowledge Tradition and Practices of India; 13. Legal Studies; 14. Environmental Science; 15.Mathematics; 16. Physical Education/NCC/Yoga; 17. Physics 18. Political Science; 19. Psychology; 20. Sociology; 21. Teaching Aptitude; 22. Agriculture; 23. Mass Media/Mass Communication; 24. Anthropology; 25. Fine Arts/Visual Arts (Sculpture/Painting)/ Commercial Arts; 26. Performing Arts – (i) Dance (Kathak/ Bharatnatyam/Oddisi/Kathakali/Kuchipudi/ Manipuri (ii) Drama-Theatre (iii) Music General (Hindustani/Carnatic/ Rabindra Sangeet/ Percussion/ Non-Percussion); 27. Sanskrit.

For all Shastri (Shastri 3 years/ 4 years Honours) Equivalent to B.A./B.A. Honours courses i.e. Shastri in Veda, Paurohitya (Karmakand), Dharamshastra, Prachin Vyakarana, Navya Vyakarana, Phalit Jyotish, Siddhant Jyotish, Vastushastra, Sahitya, Puranetihas, Prakrit Bhasha,Prachin Nyaya Vaisheshik, Sankhya Yoga, Jain Darshan, Mimansa, Advaita Vedanta, Vishihstadvaita Vedanta, Sarva Darshan, a candidate may choose Sanskrit as the Domain.

For those who are writing Sanskrit as a domain subject in Section 2, Sanskrit paper in Section 1B will be used for testing their Reading Comprehension (based on different types of passages–Factual, Literary and Narrative, [Literary Aptitude and Vocabulary].

- A Candidate can choose a maximum of **any 3 languages** from Section IA and Section IB taken together. However, the third language chosen needs to be in lieu of 6th domain specific subject chosen by the candidate - as applicable (**so the maximum number of tests to be taken remains 9 only i.e. 2 Languages+6 Domain Specific Subjects+1 General Test OR 3 Languages+5 Domain Specific Subjects+1 General Test):** Flexibility has been provided to help a candidate apply for many Universities depending on their eligibility conditions).

- Section II offers 27 subjects, out of which a candidate may choose a maximum of 6 subjects

Mode of the Test	Computer Based Test (CBT)
Test Pattern	Objective type with Multiple Choice Questions
Medium	13 languages *(Tamil, Telugu, Kannada, Malayalam, Marathi, Gujarati, Odiya, Bengali, Assamese, Punjabi, English, Hindi and Urdu)*
Syllabus	**Section IA & IB:** Language to be tested through Reading Comprehension (based on different types of passages–Factual, Literary and Narrative [Literary Aptitude & Vocabulary]
	Section II : As per NCERT model syllabus as applicable to Class XII only
	Section III : General Knowledge, Current Affairs, General Mental Ability, Numerical Ability, Quantitative Reasoning (Simple application of basic mathematical concepts arithmetic/algebra geometry/mensuration/stat taught till Grade 8), Logical and Analytical Reasoning
Registration	Registration will be online at https://cuet.samarth.ac.in/.

The candidates are advised to visit https://cuet.samarth.ac.in for more details and the registration process of the exam.

Level of questions for CUET (UG):

All questions in various testing areas will be benchmarked at the level of Class XII only. Students having studied Class XII Board syllabus would be able to do well in CUET (UG).

Each question will carry 5 marks. One mark will be deducted for a wrong answer.

Score cards will give both raw marks as well as percentile. Percentile will be calculated for each of the tests in which the candidates appeared, separately.

Number of attempts:

If any University permits students of previous years of class XII to take admission in the current year also, such students would also be eligible to appear in this year's CUET (UG).

Choice of Languages and Subjects:

Generally the languages/subjects chosen should be the ones that a student has opted in his latest Class XII Board examination. However, if any University permits any flexibility in this regards, the same can be exercised under CUET (UG) also. Candidates must carefully refer to the eligibility requirements of various Central Universities in this regard. Moreover, if the subject to be studied in the Undergraduate course is not available in the list of **27 Domain Specific Subject** being offered, the Candidate may choose the subject closest to his/her choice for e.g. For Biochemistry the candidate may choose Biology.

Wish you all the best in your CUET exam!!

Preface

It gives me immense joy and privilege to bring for my dear students and teachers my first edition of MCQ & Sample papers for CUET (UG) Business Studies. This book has been designed with utmost care adhering to the prescribed syllabus of the National Testing Agency.

During my teaching career span of 27 years. I have had the privilege to teach class XII in different schools following CBSE, ISC (CISCE) and State Boards. Due to my close interactions with students, need for quick revision and summation was perceived. MCQs could be the perfect tool to attain them.

CUET demands training of students as per the newer format of questions, whereby a student is expected to read, analyse and evaluate a given situation by logical thinking and reasoning and presenting an answer by application of one's knowledge.

This book will enrich you with:

- Key points at the beginning of each chapter for quick recapitulations.
- Complete chapter wise (Chap I to XIII) MCQs.
- Guidance regarding the question style.
  - Worksheets based on MCQs.
  - Assertion and Reasoning Questions.
  - Case Study Based Questions (MCQs).
  - Match the Column I with Column II (with MCQs).
  - Fill up the blanks (with MCQs).
- Sample Question Papers (I to III).
- All answers of MCQs of each chapter (I to XIII).
- Answers of Sample Papers I to III.
- Guidance to Crack the CUET (UG) Examination.

It is hoped that this book would prove to be a ready reckoner for students and teachers.

The feedback is always welcome to improve the book further. Suggestions can be mailed at my Email ID bindusays@gmail.com.

I take this opportunity to thank all those who have assisted me in bringing out this book.

I thank my publishers Unicorn Books, Delhi for bringing out this book in the most attractive format.

Wishing every student Best of Luck and Success in cracking CUET(UG) Examination.

Bindu Bhatia Arora

BUSINESS STUDIES – 305

Principles and Functions of Management

UNIT I: NATURE AND SIGNIFICANCE OF MANAGEMENT

- **Management** – concept, objectives, importance.
- **Nature of Management** – Management as Science, Art, Profession.
- **Levels of Management** – top, middle supervisory (First level).
- **Management Functions** – planning, organizing, staffing, directing, and controlling.
- **Coordination** – nature, and importance.

UNIT II: PRINCIPLES OF MANAGEMENT

- **Principles of Management** – meaning, nature and significance.
- Fayol's principles of management.
- **Taylor's Scientific Management** – Principles and Techniques.

UNIT III: BUSINESS ENVIRONMENT

- **Business Environment** – meaning and importance.
- **Dimensions of Business Environment** – Economic, Social, Technological, Political, and Legal.
- **Economic Environment in India** – Impact of Government policy changes on business and industry,with special reference to the adoption of the policies of liberalization privatization, and globalization.

UNIT IV: PLANNING

- Meaning, features, importance, limitations.
- Planning process.

- **Types of Plans** – Objectives, Strategy, Policy, Procedure, Method, Rule, Budget, Programme

UNIT V: ORGANISING

- Meaning and importance.
- Steps in the process of organizing.
- Structure of organization – functional, and divisional.
- Formal and informal organization.
- Delegation: meaning elements and importance.
- Decentralization: meaning and importance.
- Difference between delegation and decentralization.

UNIT VI: STAFFING

- Meaning, need, and importance of staffing.
- Staffing as a part of Human Resources Management.
- Steps in the staffing process.
- **Recruitment** – meaning and sources.
- **Selection** – meaning and process.
- **Training and Development** – meaning, need, **methods** – on the job and off the job methods of training.

UNIT VII: DIRECTING

- Meaning, importance, and principles.
- **Elements of Direction:**
  - **Supervision** – meaning and importance
  - **Motivation** – meaning and importance, Maslow's hierarchy of needs; Financial and non-financial incentives.
  - **Leadership** – meaning, importance; qualities of a good leader.

- **Communication –** meaning and importance, formal and informal communication; barriers to effective communication.

UNIT VIII: CONTROLLING

- Meaning and Importance.
- Relationship between planning and controlling.
- Steps in the process of control.
- Techniques of controlling.

Business Finance and Marketing

UNIT IX: BUSINESS FINANCE

- **Business Finance –** meaning, role, objectives of financial management.
- **Financial Planning –** meaning and importance.
- **Capital Structure –** meaning and factors.
- **Fixed and Working Capital –** meaning and factors affecting their requirements.

UNIT X: FINANCIAL MARKETS

- **Concept of Financial Market: Money Market –** nature instruments;
- **Capital Market: Nature and Types –** primary and secondary market.
- The distinction between capital market and money market.
- **Stock Exchange –** meaning, functions, NSEI, OCTEI, Trading Procedure.
- **Securities and Exchange Board of India (SEBI) –** Objectives, Functions.

UNIT XI: MARKETING

- **Marketing –** meaning, functions, role.
- The distinction between marketing and selling.
- **Marketing Mix –** concept and elements:
  - **Product –** nature, classification, branding, labeling, and packaging

- **Physical Distribution:** meaning, role; Channels of Distribution, – meaning, types, factors, determining the choice of channels.
- **Promotion –** meaning and role, promotion mix, Role of Advertising and personal selling; objections to Advertising.
- **Price:** factors influencing pricing.

UNIT XII: CONSUMER PROTECTION

- Importance of consumer protection.
- Consumer rights.
- Consumer responsibilities.
- **Ways and means of consumer protection –** Consumer awareness and legal redressal with special reference to the Consumer Protection Act.
- Role of consumer organizations and NGOs.

UNIT XIII: ENTREPRENEURSHIP DEVELOPMENT

- Concept, Functions, and Need.
- Entrepreneurship Characteristics and Competencies.
- Process of Entrepreneurship Development.
- Entrepreneurial Values, Attitudes, and Motivation – Meaning and Concept.

Contents

Nature and Significance of Management

KEY POINTS

- ➤ **Management Concept**
  - Effectiveness vs Efficiency
- ➤ **Characteristics of Management**
  - Management is Goal Oriented
  - Management is All Pervasive
  - Management is Multidimensional
  - Management is a Continuous Process
  - Management is a Group Activity
  - Management is a Dynamic Function
  - Management is an Intangible Force
- ➤ **Objectives of Management**
  - Personnel
  - Social
  - Organisational Objectives
- ➤ **Importance of Management**
  - Achieving Group Goals
  - Increases Efficiency
  - Creates a Dynamic Organisation
  - Helps in Achieving Personal Objectives
  - Helps in the Development of Society
- ➤ **Nature of Management**
  - Management as Profession
  - Management as Science
  - Management as Art
- ➤ **Levels of Management**

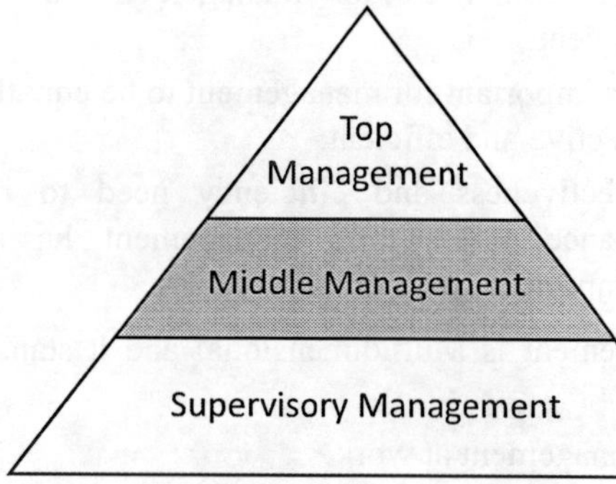

- ➤ **Functions of Management**

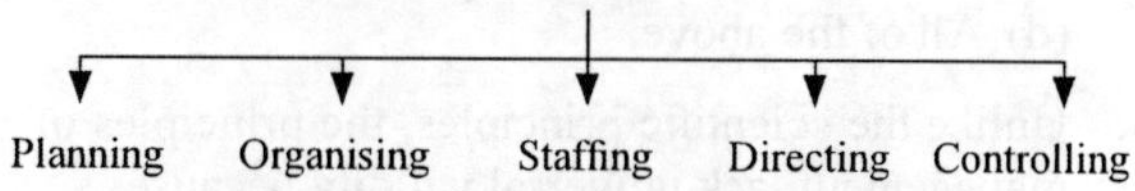

- ➤ **Co-ordination – Essence of Management**
  - **Characteristics**
    - (i) Integrates Group Efforts
    - (ii) Ensures Unity of Action
    - (iii) Continuous Process
    - (iv) All Pervasive Function
    - (v) Responsibility of All Managers
    - (vi) Deliberate Function
  - **Importance**
    - (i) Growth in Size
    - (ii) Functional Differentiation
    - (iii) Specialisation
- ➤ **Management in Global Perspective**

MCQs

1. It is important for management to achieve goals with minimum resources. It means that
   (a) It is important for management to be effective.
   (b) It is important for management to be efficient.
   (c) It is important for management to be equally effective and efficient.
   (d) Effectiveness and efficiency need to be balanced and at times management has to compromise with efficiency .
2. Management is Multidimensional and it stands for
   (a) Management at work.
   (b) Management of people.
   (c) Management of operations.
   (d) All of the above.
3. Unlike the scientific principles, the principles of management lack universal validity because
   (a) Principles are based on personal observation.
   (b) They deal with human behaviour which is complex in nature.
   (c) Management is a complete art of getting work done.
   (d) All of the above.
4. Supervisory management plays a very important role in the organisation since
   (a) They interact and pass on instructions to the actual force.
   (b) They interpret the policies framed by the top management.
   (c) They are responsible for the welfare and survival of the organisation .
   (d) None of the above.
5. "The activities of a manager are inter-related", the above statement relates to the
   (a) Functions of management.
   (b) Organisation of activities.
   (c) Staffing of workforce.
   (d) Operational Management.
6. "It bridges the gap between where we are and where we want to go", the function is
   (a) Planning (b) Organising
   (c) Staffing (d) Directing
7. In this function the manager tries to match the actual performance with the planned performance.
   (a) Planning (b) Organising
   (c) Staffing (d) Controlling
8. Co-ordination is
   (a) Function of management.
   (b) The essence of management.
   (c) Objective of management.
   (d) None of the above.
9. Today, the role of global managers has evolved. They should have
   (a) Diverse combination of technical skills.
   (b) Soft management and people skills.
   (c) The ability to imbibe and learn different cultural experiences.
   (d) All of the above.
10. The complexities of modern technology and diversity of tasks to be performed leads to
    (a) Co-ordination (b) Specialisation
    (c) Management (d) None of the above
11. Management as an Art has the following feature
    (a) Theoretical knowledge and personalised application.
    (b) Universal validity.
    (c) Systematic body of knowledge
    (d) None of the above.
12. Mc Donald's the fast food giant made major changes in menu to be able to survive in the Indian market. This highlights which characteristics of Management?
    (a) Management is an intangible force

(b) Management is a group activity

(c) Management is a dynamic function

(d) Management is all pervasive.

13. Which of this is not the primary function of a management?

(a) Planning (b) Co-ordination

(c) Staffing (d) Directing

14. Which of these is not a characteristics of a profession?

(a) Professional association

(b) Ethical code of conduct

(c) Service Motive

(d) Open entry

15. Division heads are seen in

(a) Operational management

(b) Middle management

(c) Top management

(d) All of the above

16. "Right people for Right Job" is a

(a) Directing function

(b) Staffing function

(c) Controlling function

(d) Organising function

17. The key components of Directing function is

(a) Motivation (b) Leadership

(c) Communication (d) All of the above

18. Unity of Action in the realisation of common purpose is achieved through

(a) Co-operation (b) Motivation

(c) Co-ordination (d) Direction

19. The world as a 'global village' means

(a) The scope of international relationship is expanding

(b) It has to be managed in global perspective

(c) The inter cultural relationship is rapidly expanding

(d) All of the above

20. Which function establishes 'Reporting Relationship'

(a) Planning (b) Organising

(c) Staffing (d) Directing

21. 'Together everyone achieves more as a Team' because

(a) Management is a process

(b) Management is a group activity

(c) Management is a continuous process

(d) Management is intangible

22. Rajiv has achieved a target of producing 500 units, though at a higher cost. He is

(a) Efficient

(b) Effective

(c) Both Efficient and Effective

(d) None of the above

23. Which level of management is responsible for the welfare and survival of the Organisation?

(a) Top level Management

(b) Middle level Management

(c) Supervisory level

(d) Both (b) & (c) above

24. "Management is required in all kinds of organisation - Business or Non Business." This is highlighted in which of the below mentioned characteristics

(a) Multi-dimensional (b) All pervasive

(c) Goal Oriented (d) All of the above

25. The task of management is to make people work towards achieving the organisation's goals by making their strengths effective and their weaknesses irrelevant. This highlights the dimension of

(a) Management of work

(b) Management of people

(c) Management of operations

(d) (a) & (c) above

26. By using environment friendly methods of production, earthen coolers are manufactured by a small company. This fulfills which of the below mentioned management objective of the company?

(a) Social objective

(b) Personal objective

(c) Organisational objective
(d) Economic objective

27. Successful organisations do not achieve their goals by chance but by following a deliberate process called
(a) Effectiveness (b) Efficiency
(c) Coordination (d) Management

28. The presence of management in any organisation can be felt not seen. This can be observed by
(a) Systematic working
(b) Orderliness and coordination in the working environment
(c) (a) & (b) above
(d) None of the above

29. "What distinguishes a successful manager from a less successful one, is the ability to put the principles into practice". Which aspect of the nature of management is highlighted by the above statement?
(a) Management as a Science
(b) Management as an Art
(c) Management as a Profession
(d) Management as an Intangible force

30. Good manager not only focuses on prosperity of management but he also focuses on prosperity of employees. Which point of importance is highlighted here?
(a) Management helps in achieving organisation's goal.
(b) Management creates dynamic organisation.
(c) Management improves efficiency.
(d) Management helps in achieving personal goals.

31. In absence of management, resources.
(a) Never become production.
(b) Cannot be used effectively.
(c) Cannot be used efficiently.
(d) All of the above.

32. A leading company started a school nearby for the children of their employees. Identify the objective, company is fulfilling
(a) Social objective.
(b) Personal objective.
(c) Social & personal objective.
(d) Organisational objective.

33. Management is called process because it involves
(a) Co-ordination.
(b) Series of functions.
(c) Achieving Multiple objectives.
(d) All of the above.

34. One of the organisational objectives of Management is 'Growth of a business', which one of the following is not associated to measurement of business growth?
(a) Sales volume
(b) Number of Employees
(c) Number of products offered
(d) Number of Creditors.

35. Geeta is working at the top level of management in the private sector bank. Which of these functions she has to perform?
(a) She is responsible for all the business activities and its impact on society
(b) She has to co-ordinate the activities of different departments
(c) She is responsible for the success and failure of the organisation.
(d) All of the above.

36. Assertion (A): The role of global manager has evolved in the same way as global industry and economy.

Reason (R): Global Manager has a multifaceted role, which requires diverse combination of skills:

(a) Both (A) and (R) are true
(b) Both (A) and (R) are false
(c) (A) is true and (R) is false
(d) (A) is false and (R) is true

CHAPTER 2

Principles of Management

KEY POINTS

- **Meaning, Nature of Management Principles Contribution of F. W. Taylor (American Mechanical Engineer) and Henri Fayol (French Mining Engineer)**
- **Nature of Principles of Management**
  - Universal applicability
  - General guidelines
  - Formed by practice and experience
  - Flexible
  - Mainly behavioural
  - Cause and effect relationship
  - Contingent
- **Significance of Principles of Management**
  - Social Responsibility
  - Providing managers with useful insights into reality
  - Optimum utilization of resources
  - Scientific decisions
  - Adapt to dynamic environment
  - Management training education and research
- **Principles of Scientific Management**
  - Science not Rule of thumb
  - Harmony not Discord
  - Cooperation not Individualism
  - Development of manpower
- **Techniques of Scientific Management**
  - Functional foremanship
  - Differential piece wage system
  - Standardisation of work
  - Time study
  - Method study
  - Motion study
  - Fatigue study
- **Mental Revolution**
- **Fayol's Principles of Management**
  - Division of Work
  - Centralisation and Decentralisation
  - Authority & Responsibility
  - Scalar Chain
  - Discipline
  - Order
  - Unity of Command
  - Equity
  - Unity of Direction
  - Stability of Personnel
  - Remuneration of Employees
  - Initiative
  - Subordination of Individual interest to general interest
  - Esprit De Corps
- **Fayol vs Taylor: a comparison**
  - Complementary
  - Points of difference

MCQs

1. The effect of managerial principles varies from one situation to another situation. This is because it is related to one of the following characteristics of management principles:
   (a) Cause and effect relationship
   (b) Universal application
   (c) Flexible
   (d) Contingent

2. 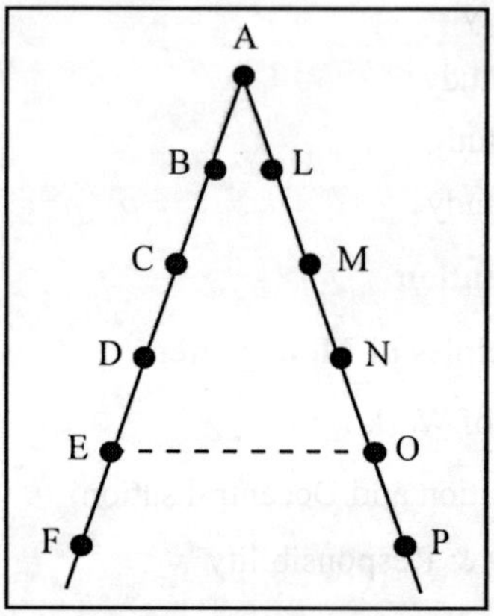

   This diagram refers to Fayol's principle of Scalar Chain which talks about:
   (a) Chain of authority and communication.
   (b) Need to balance subordinate involvement through decentralisation.
   (c) All units of an organisation should be moving towards the same objective.
   (d) Chain of authority and responsibility.

3. The principle of management can be changed according to the prevailing situation in an organisation. This shows that management principles are
   (a) Behavioural (b) Flexible
   (c) Scientific (d) Universal

4. Henri Fayol was:-
   (a) Social Scientist
   (b) Mining Engineer
   (c) Mechanical Engineer
   (d) Production Engineer

5. The Principles of management are developed on the basis of:
   (a) Experiences of customers
   (b) Propagation of social scientist
   (c) Experimentation in laboratory
   (d) Observation and experiences of managers

6. Now-a-days in multinational corporation people of various nationalities work together in a discrimination free environment. This highlights Fayol's principle of:
   (a) Stability of Personnel
   (b) Equity
   (c) Unity of Command
   (d) Discipline

7. Rest intervals in job helps in increasing productivity. They are decided By:
   (a) Motion study (b) Fatigue study
   (c) Method study (d) Time study

8. Panchayats in our country have been given more powers to decide and spend funds granted to them by the government for welfare of villages. Identify the principles of management highlighted in this statement:
   (a) Authority and Responsibility
   (b) Esprit De Corps
   (c) Equity
   (d) Centralisation and Decentralisation

9. Functional foremanship is the extension of which principle of management:
   (a) Unity of Direction (b) Discipline
   (c) Division of work (d) Unity of command

10. According to Fayol a manager should replace 'I' with 'We' in all his conversations with workers to foster team spirit, otherwise:
    (a) a feeling of mistrust grows among team members
    (b) Realising of objectives would be difficult
    (c) there will be loss of co-ordination
    (d) all of the above

11. Taylor believed that efficiency can be maximised through study and analysis. Identify the principle of scientific management meant above:

[CBSE sample paper 2021-22]

(a) Harmony not discord

(b) Science not rule of thumb

(c) Co-operation not Individualism

(d) Development of each and every person to his or her greatest efficiency and prosperity

12. According to the technique of scientific Management i.e. 'Differential Piece Wage System', how much more will a worker making 60 units earn, as compared to a worker making 49 units, if the standard output per day is 50 units and those who make standard output or more than standard, get Rs. 75 per unit and those below get Rs. 65 per unit?

[CBSE sample paper 2021-22]

(a) Rs. 4500 (b) Rs. 1315

(c) Rs. 3185 (d) Rs. 3250

13. Which of the following statement best describes 'Mental Revolution'?

(i) It implies change of attitude

(ii) The Management and workers should co-operate and not compete.

(iii) Management should share a part of the surplus with workers.

(a) (i) & (ii) (b) (ii) & (iii)

(c) (iii) & (i) above (d) all of the above

14. Sagar and Riya are two young MBA graduates. Together They joined the same company.

Their manager Radha wants to give more and better opportunities to Riya so that a female employee grows faster in career. Which principle of management is being violated in this case:

(a) Principle of Discipline

(b) Principle of Equity

(c) Principle of Authority & Responsibility

(d) All of the above

15. Fayol first identified these functions of management:

(a) Planning, Organising, Staffing, Directing

(b) Plan, Organise, Command, Co-ordinate and Control

(c) Planning, Organising, Controlling, Directing

(d) Planning, Organising, Directing and Co-operating

16. Indo Engineering Ltd. is a production house of small tools and machines. They feel the success of their company is lot due to use of Scientific Management technique called "Lean Manufacturing". Which of the following are the outcomes of Lean Manufacturing?

(a) A systematic method of waste minimization

(b) Methods enhancing the quality of output

(c) Methods that help in reduction of cost due to reduced production time

(d) All of the above

17. Fayol developed this concept of administration and propounded certain principles. These principles are ________ in number:

(a) 15 (b) 12

(c) 14 (d) 13

18. The person who keeps machines, materials, tools etc ready for operations for concerned workers, under functional foreman-ship, is called:

(a) Instruction Card Clerk

(c) Gang Boss

(b) Time and Cost Clerk

(d) Route Clerk

19. Which of the following methods has helped Microsoft company the most to have attained large share in market for their products?

(a) Method study

(b) Simplification and standardisation of work

(c) Functional foreman-ship

(d) All of the above

20. Which one of the following principles is an extension of 'Harmony not Discord'?

(a) Principle of Science not Rule of thumb

(b) Co operation not Individualism

(c) Development of workers to their greatest efficiency.

(d) None of the above.

21. Name the Fayol's principle of management which minimizes employee's turnover.

(a) Equity

(b) Fair Remuneration

(c) Stability of tenure of personnel

(d) Subordination of Individual interest to General interest

22. Today certain new & modern scientific techniques are developed and used in companies. Which one of the following is not a sequel to scientific management?

(a) Operations Research (b) Kaizen

(c) Six Sigma (d) Esprit de corps

23. Gang plank permits direct communication between

(a) Employees working at same level

(b) Any employees irrespective of their level

(c) Employees of same department only

(d) None of the above

24. The foreman responsible for quality of work is

(a) Disciplinarian (b) Repair Boss

(c) Inspector (d) Gang Boss

25. Name the technique of Taylor which acts as the strongest motivator for workers to reach standard performance.

(a) Method Study

(b) Differential piece rate system

(c) Time Study

(d) Motion Study

26. In Japanese Companies 'Paternalist Style of Management is in practice. This means that there is.

(a) Complete openness between Management and workers.

(b) Employers take care of the needs of the employees.

(c) Trade Unions are not required

(d) All of the above

27. 'Dual Subordination' should be avoided. The consequences of this are:

(a) Confusion and Indiscipline

(b) Ego clashes among different superiors

(c) Both (a) and (b) above

(d) None of the above

28. A private school in a city started extra coaching classes for the students of Class-XII after the official school hours. For this they took extra fees from the students,over and above their regular tuition fee.

For this purpose, some teachers had to stay back after duty hours and give extra hours of teaching. However the school refused to pay them any extra money for extra work. Which principle was violated by them?

(a) Remuneration of employees

(b) Equity

(c) Discipline

(d) Subordination of individual interest to General interest

29. When the principle of Remuneration is violated the consequences are

(a) Confusion and indiscipline

(b) Demotivation of employees

(c) Increase in commitment in employees

(d) No achievement of organisation goals

30. Which statement best describes the principle of Division of Work?

(i) Work should be divided into small tasks.

(ii) Labour should be divided

(iii) Resources should be divided into jobs.

(iv) It leads to specialisation.

Choose the right answer:

(a) (i) & (ii) above (b) (ii) & (iii) above

(c) (iii) & (iv) above (d) (i) & (iv) above

31. Principle of Initiatives should be encouraged in organisations because it

(a) develops the feeling of belongingness in employees

(b) boosts up the morale of employees

(c) Employees try to achieve targets on time
(d) All of the above

32. A salesman of A B Engineering Ltd. could not achieve his sales target of 10,000 units. On enquiry it was found that he was not allowed to take decisions related to give discount and selling on credit to any of his customers. The principle of management which is violated here is:-
(a) Discipline
(b) Authority and Responsibility
(c) Centralisation and Decentralisation
(d) Principle of Order.

33. A sales person is allowed to close a deal with a buyer giving maximum discount @5% whereas decision regarding any further discount on Puja/ festivals rests with the Sales Manager as a final authority. Identify the principle of Management which is being followed here:-
(a) Centralisation and Decentralisation
(b) Unity of Command
(c) Authority and Responsibility
(d) Unity of Direction

34. Taylor & Fayol's principles are complementary to each other. However, they had different theories in one of the following principles:
(a) Unity of direction
(b) Unity of command
(c) Co-operation not Individualism
(d) Authority and Responsibility

35. Taylor proposed eight specialists from whom each worker will have to take orders from as part of the technique of Functional Foremanship specified by him. Those with technical mastery, intelligence and grit may be given __________ work. Those with energy and good health may be assigned __________ work.
(a) Planning, Execution
(b) Execution, planning
(c) Production, planning
(d) Implementation, production.

36. Assertion (A): Management principles are not as rigid as principles of pure science.
Reason (R): Human Behaviour is never static and so also technology, which affects business.
(a) Both (A) and (R) are correct
(b) (A) is correct (R) is incorrect
(c) Both (A) and (R) are correct and (R) is the correct explanation of (A)
(d) Both (A) & (R) are correct and (R) is not the correct explanation of (A)

37. Assertion (A) Personnel should be selected and appointed after rigorous procedure .
Once selected they should be kept in post for a minimum fixed tenure.
Reason (R) Any adhocism in this regard will create instability among employees.
(a) Both (A) and (R) are correct.
(b) A is correct and (R) is incorrect.
(c) Both (A) and (R) are correct and (R) is the correct explanation of A.
(d) Both (A) and (R) are correct and (R) is not the correct explanation of A.

CHAPTER 3

Business Environment

KEY POINTS

- **Meaning of Business Environment**
  - Totality of external forces
  - Specific and general factors
  - Inter relatedness
  - Uncertainty
  - Dynamic nature
  - Complexity
  - Relativity
- **Importance of Business Environment**
  - First mover advantage
  - Identify threats and warning signals
  - Tapping useful resources
  - Coping with rapid changes
  - Assists on planning and policy formulation
  - Improving performance
- **Elements/Dimensions of Business Environment**
  - Economic
  - Social
  - Legal
  - Technological
  - Poltical
- **Economic Environment in India**

  Factors which can have impact on business and Industry
  - Stage of economic development of the country
  - Economic structure in the form of mixed economy
  - Economic policies of the Government
  - Economic planning
  - Economic Indices
  - Infrastructural factors
- **New Industrial Policy (1991)**
  - Liberalisation
  - Privatisation
  - Globalisation
  - Automatic permission granted for technology agreements with foreign companies.
  - Foreign Investment promotion Board was setup.
- **Demonetisation**
- **Impact of Government Policy Changes on Business and Industry**
  - Loss of budgetary support to the public sector
  - Need for developing human resource
  - Increasing competition
  - Demanding customers
  - Changing technological environment
  - Market orientation
  - Necessity for change

MCQs

1. Which of the following is not a feature of Business Environment?
   (a) Different elements of business environment are closely interrelated.
   (b) Business Environment is dynamic.
   (c) Business Environment is a simple phenomenon and easy to understand.
   (d) Business environment is uncertain as it is difficult to predict future happenings.
2. A smart manager identifies the threat/warning signals to survive in market. Which of the following measures can be adopted by them to survive?
   (a) Improve the quality of product
   (b) Reduce the cost of product
   (c) Engage aggressive advertising
   (d) All of the above
3. The organic food market in India is growing at a rate of 25% - 30%. This reflects a clear shift in consumers taste and preference. Identify the feature of business environment being referred here: (I) Dynamic nature (II) Inter-relatedness (III) Relativity

   Choose the right answer below:
   (a) Points (I) & (II) above
   (b) Points (II) & (III) above
   (c) Points (I) & (III) above
   (d) All of the above
4. Manish Confectioneries was earlier supplying bakery products in one locality in N. Delhi. Now with the changing trend and consumption habits of the people of that locality, they extended and modernized it into a cafe by the name of 'Coffee and Cake Cafe' with a smart air conditioned Sit-in-area. They, along with bakery products, also included certain popular snacks and coffee.
   (I) Identify the element of business environment discussed above:
   (a) Social Environment
   (b) Political Environment
   (c) Legal Environment
   (d) Economic Environment
   (II) Coffee and Cake Cafe also created their website and started taking online orders.

   They got lot of orders online and earned good profits by selling their products.

   Identify the business environment discussed in above case.
   (a) Economic Environment
   (b) Technological Environment
   (c) Social Environment
   (d) Legal Environment
5. Values refers to concepts that a society holds in high esteem. Which one of the following is not an example of a value in business world?
   (a) Freedom of choice in market
   (b) Social justice
   (c) Discriminatory employment
   (d) Equality of opportunity
6. Proper understanding and awareness about the business environment brings lot of benefits for the businessmen. Which of the following best indicates the importance of business environment?
   (a) Get First Mover advantage
   (b) To identify early warning signals
   (c) Adjust and adapt with rapid changes
   (d) All of the above
7. This Online and 'Work from home' culture globally has helped many firms to remain in market and carry on their tasks. This is related to:
   (a) Political Environment
   (b) Social Environment
   (c) Technological Environment
   (d) Economic Environment
8. The nature of the relationship of one country with other countries is a direct reflection on:
   (a) Social Environment
   (b) Political Environment
   (c) Legal Environment

(d) Economic environment

9. Demonetisation of Rs. 500 and Rs. 1000 notes by the Prime Minister of India had its impact on which dimension of business environment

(a) Political (b) Legal
(c) Economic (d) Technological

10. It is compulsory for companies to advertise that "Cigarette smoking is injurious to health" as a statutory warning. This is highlighted in:

(a) Social Environment
(b) Political Environment
(c) Economic Environment
(d) Legal environment

11. On scanning the Indian Business Environment one finds that there is a great scope of Tourism Industry in our country. This is highlighted in which of the following points of importance:

(a) Assisting in planning & policy making
(b) Improvement in performance
(c) Helpful in tapping and assembling resources
(d) Helpful to adapt changes

12. Performance of a business enterprises is not only affected by forces within but also by forces outside the boundaries of the organisation. These forces may be:

(a) Goverment Policies
(b) Technological Developments
(c) Political Stability
(d) All of the above

13. ABZ Manufacturing Ltd. Co. changed their hiring policy. They now hire at least 50% women for any post in their organisation. Which dimension of business environment is highlighted here?

(a) Political (b) Legal
(c) Social (d) Technological

14. New Industrial Policy of 1991 aimed to liberate the industry from the shackles of Licensing system, which of the below mentioned points does not belong to this?

(a) Reduction in the role of public sector
(b) Encouragement of foreign direct participation
(c) Requirement of permission for technology agreement with foreign countries
(d) Reduction of industries under compulsory licensing

15. Relaxation or removal of strict rules and regulations is part of

(a) Liberalisation (b) Privatisation
(c) Globalisation (d) All of the above

16. Aiming to revive Jammu & Kashmir's attraction as a top location for film shooting, the J & K film policy, 2021 offers a host of incentives to the film makers such as subsidies, long term loans with low interest rates,esp for films with patriotic and certain other themes and for giving work opportunities to local artists etc. This will have an impact on the business enterprises in the State. Which component of business environment is highlighted above?

(a) Specific &General forces
(b) Economic environment
(c) Technological Environment
(d) Totality of External forces

17. In a small town of UP, Ram Kishore has a factory of Readymade garments. He has 15 labour force for stitching clothes for ladies and children . When the 2nd wave of Coronavirus came and lockdown was announced, he immediately realised that his regular demand will get affected. Immediately He switched and directed his team to stitch PPE kits and Masks etc for healthcare sector instead of garments. This way he saved himself for going into loss and also could meet the current demand of his customers. The above case highlights one of the points related to the importance of the Business environment. Business Enviornment—

(a) helps in coping with rapid change.
(b) helps the firm to improve their performance
(c) helps the firm to identify threats and warning signals.
(d) enables the firm to identify opportunities and getting the first mover advantage.

18. Government's attempt to make 'Cash Lite' economy means:

(a) Channelling more Savings through the formal financial system.
(b) Improving tax compliance
(c) Both (a) & (b) above

(d) None of the above

19. Liberalisation means:
    (a) Integration among economies.
    (b) Reduced government controls & restrictions.
    (c) Policy of planned disinvestments.
    (d) None of the above.

20. Impact of Demonetisation was noticed in various areas of Indian Economy. Which one of the following area does not highlight this:
    (a) Private wealth (b) Public sector wealth
    (c) Digitisation (d) Real Estate

21. Government of India made announcement of demonetisation of 500/- & 1000/- Rupee notes on
    (a) 8th Nov. 2016 (b) 10th Nov. 2016
    (c) 9th Nov. 2016 (d) 7th Nov. 2016

22. With the policy of Liberalisation, privatisation and globalisation significant changes are seen in the working of business organisations. Today companies follow marketing concepts. This means that:
    (a) Firms have to study and analyses the market first and produce goods accordingly.
    (b) Firms have to produce their products and search for its market.
    (c) Firms have to modify the demands of customers.
    (d) None of the above.

23. Which of the following does not explain the impact of government policy changes on business & industry?
    (a) More demanding customer
    (b) Increase in competition
    (c) Change in agricultural prices
    (d) Market orientation

24. Today, it is essential that Public sector undertakings become more efficient to survive and grow. The reason for this is
    (a) Loss of government budgetary support for financing
    (b) They may face disinvestment
    (c) Both (a) & (b)
    (d) None of the above

25. India adopted a policy of Globalisation which means the whole world becomes a global village. The measures taken by the government to adopt this was:
    (a) Import Liberalisation
    (b) Replacement of FERA to FEMA
    (c) Rationalization of Tariff structure
    (d) All of the above

26. To execute the policy of privatisation government took the following steps:
    (i) Disinvestments of public sector
    (ii) Setting up of BIFR
    (iii) Dilution of Stake of Govt.

    Choose the right answer:
    (a) Only (i) & (ii) above
    (b) (i), (ii) & (iii) above
    (c) (ii) & (iii) above
    (d) (i) & (iii) above

27. Business Environment is the sum-total of all factors and forces ________ to a business.
    (a) specific (b) external
    (c) internal (d) all of the above

28. Match the following:

	Column I		Column II
A.	Need for developing human resource	(i)	Globalisation
B.	Rapidly changing technological environment	(ii)	Economic Environment
C.	Zero Defect Zero Effect Model has link	(iii)	People with higher competence and greater commitment
D.	Stock Market indicates	(iv)	Tough challenge for small firms

Choose the correct answer:

(a) A (i), B (iii), C (iv), D (ii)
(b) A (iii), B (iv), C (i), D (ii)
(c) A (iv), B (ii), C (iii), D (i)
(d) A (ii), B (iii), C (i), D (iv)

CHAPTER 4

Planning

KEY POINTS

- **Planning Concept and Importance**
  - Planning provides directions
  - Planning reduces the risk of uncertainty
  - Planning reduces overlapping and wasteful activities
  - Planning promotes innovative ideas
  - Planning facilitates decision making
  - Planning establishes standards for controlling
- **Features of Planning**
  - Achieving objective
  - Primary function
  - Mental Exercise
  - All pervasive
  - Decision making
  - Continuous
  - Futuristic
- **Limitations of Planning**
  - Leads to rigidity
  - May not work in a dynamic environment
  - Reduces creativity
  - Involves huge costs
  - Time consuming
  - Does not guarantee success
- **Planning Process**
  - Setting objectives
  - Developing premises
  - Identifying alternatives action
  - Evaluating alternatives
  - Selecting an alternative
  - Implementing the plan
  - Follow up
- **Type of Plan**
  - Single Use
  - Standing Plan
- **Types of Plans**
  - Strategy
  - Objectives
  - Policy
  - Procedure
  - Methods
  - Rule
  - Programme
  - Budget

MCQs

1. "Planning is concerned with both ends and means"

   This statements means:

   (a) Setting of objectives and targets of a company

   (b) Formulating of an action plan for achievement of goals.

   (c) Ends and Means is same thing.

   (d) Both (a) & (b) above

2. All Managers in order to be successful in their businesses need to think seriously , work hard and then make business predictions.

   Above statement describes one of the below mentioned concepts – Identify it

   (a) Management (b) Co-ordination

   (c) Specialisation (d) Planning

3. Planning is the pre requisite for controlling .This statement means:

   (a) The nature of corrective action depends upon the extent of deviation.

   (b) Planning provides the basis of control.

   (c) Controlling comes after the planning stage

   (d) All of the above.

4. Business environment is dynamic but good heads in planning department do not get shocked with sudden changes.

   This highlights which of these point of importance of planning

   (a) Planning facilitates decision making

   (b) Planning promotes innovative ideas.

   (c) Planning reduces risk of uncertainties

   (d) Planning provide direction

5. Planning requires logical and systematic thinking. The feature of planning referred here is:

   (a) Routine activity (b) Mental exercise

   (c) Continuous process (d) All pervasive

6. 'Planning cannot foresee everything', which of these are obstacles for effective planning?

   (a) Competition in market

   (b) Political condition in the country

   (c) Natural calamity.

   (d) All of the above.

7. ____________ provides a rational approach for setting objectives and developing appropriate courses of action for achieving predetermined objectives.

   (a) Directing (b) Staffing

   (c) Planning (d) Controlling

8. The statement "Planning is a primary function" suggests that ____________

   (a) Planning precedes other function

   (b) Planning requires logical and systematic thinking.

   (c) Plan is framed ,it is implemented and is followed by another plan, and so on

   (d) Planning is required at all levels of Management as well as in all departments of the organisation.

9. Employees have to follow plans totally. This way planning reduces

   (a) Creativity of workers

   (b) Interest in organisation

   (c) Application of knowledge

   (d) None of the above.

10. The retirement age of employees is 60 years in a Company. This is a ____________ of a Company.

    (a) Strategy (b) Policy

    (c) Rule (d) Procedure

11. Identify the correct statement:

    Statement I: Planning does not guarantee success.

    Statement II: Manager cannot afford to be complacent to follow an earlier tested plan.

    Choose the right answer:

    (a) Both statement I & II is correct.

(b) Only statement I is correct and II is wrong.
(c) Only statement II is correct and I is wrong.
(d) Both statements are wrong.

12. Planning is closely connected with ____________ and ____________
(a) Responsibility & accountability
(b) Delegation & Decentralisation
(c) Stability and security
(d) Creativity and Innovation.

13. Which step in the process of planning will precede the step in which, the manager is required to make certain assumptions about the future, which are the base material upon which the plans are drawn.
(a) Implementing the plan.
(b) Setting objectives
(c) Identifying alternative course of action.
(d) Selecting an alternative.

14. Following a pre-decided plan, when circumstances change, they may not turn out in the organisation's interest .
The limitation of planning being referred to in the above statement is ____________
(a) Planning does not guarantee success.
(b) Planning may not work in dynamic environment.
(c) Planning leads to rigidity.
(d) Planning is time consuming process.

15. "The cost incurred in planning sometimes does not justify the benefit derived for the plans" This is because:
(a) There are number of incidental cost which were not planned.
(b) Huge costs are incurred to make a scientific plan but still viability of the plans may change due to unforeseen factors.
(c) It is important to find the viability of plan.
(d) More than required expenses are incurred to make plans.

16. "Goods sold for cash only. No credit please". This statement highlights a particular type of plan which is
(a) Single use plan
(b) Standing Plan
(c) Neither single use nor standing plan
(d) General plan.

17. Assertion (A): Planning is futuristic .
Reason (R): Planning is concerned with the future which is certain and does not require forecast. [CBSE Sample Paper 2021-22]
(a) Both (A) & (R) are correct
(b) (A) is correct and (R) is incorrect
(c) Both (A) and (R) are correct and (R) is the correct explanation of (A)
(d) Both (A) & (R) are correct and R is not the correct explanation of (A).

18. Match the terms in Column I with suitable narration in Column II:

	Column I		Column II
I	Policy	A.	Advertisement of BYJU coaching during Tata IPL cricket matches.
II	Procedure	B.	Keeping two passport size photographs along with duly filled admission form in the admission file of the candidate.
III	Strategy	C.	All mobiles to be switched off during formal office meetings.
IV	Rule	D.	Students who secure 70% in class X board exams are eligible to get admission in Class XI Science.

Choose the correct pairs
(a) I-A, II-C, III-B, IV-D
(b) I-D, II-B, III-A, IV-C
(c) I-B, II-A, III-D, IV-C
(d) I-C, II-D, III-A, IV-B

19. Planning is a continuous process so monitoring of plans while it is getting implemented is very essential. This highlights which step of planning process:

(a) Evaluation of different alternatives
(b) Selecting of alternatives
(c) Follow up
(d) Implementing the plan

20. Derivative plans are must for accomplishing the objective of main plan. They are seen in which step of planning process
(a) Follow up
(b) Developing premises
(c) Evaluation of different alternatives
(d) Selecting of alternatives

21. An accountant in a firm was provided with the list of areas where he was to follow straight line method or Reducing balance method of depreciation. This is related to which type of plan:
(a) Procedure (b) Strategy
(c) Methods (d) Policy

22. Assertion (A) Budget is a statement of expected results expressed in numerical term.
Reason (R) A budget is a controlling devise from which deviation can be taken care of
(a) Both (A) and (R) are not correct.
(b) (A) is correct and (R) is incorrect.
(c) (A) and (R) are correct and (R) is not the correct explanation of A.
(d) (A) and (R) are correct and (R) is the correct explanation of A.

23. 'Objectives of a firm need to be expressed in specific terms'. This statement means that objectives should be:
(a) Measurable in quantitative terms.
(b) It should be in the form of written statement of desired results to be acheived
(c) Time period to achieve objectives should be provided beforehand.
(d) All of the above.

24. Pet animals are not allowed in some eatery joints and cafes. This is related to which type of plan.
(a) Strategy (b) Policy
(c) Rule (d) Objective

25. Employees have to follow plans totally. This way planning reduces
(a) Creativity of workers
(b) Interest in company
(c) Application of knowledge
(d) None of the above

26. ________________ reduces overlapping and wasteful activities.
(a) Organisation (b) Planning
(c) Specialisation (d) Procedure

27. Managers spend a lot of time and money to formulate a plan. Which one of these is not a feature of an Ideal plan:
(a) It should be goal oriented
(b) It must be futuristic
(c) It may not work in dynamic environment.
(d) It must be a continuous process.

28. 'Swachh Bharat Abhiyan' started by government of India is an example of which type of plan?
(a) Policy (b) Objective
(c) Programme (d) Rules

29. Single use plans are
(a) used only once
(b) used by single individual
(c) used for one single department
(d) All of the above

30. What are certain assumptions about the future on the basis of which the plan are ultimately formulated?
(a) Management premises
(b) Planning premises
(c) Esteem needs
(d) Method premises

CHAPTER 5

Organising

KEY POINTS

➤ **Meaning and Process**
- Identification and division of work
- Departmentalisation
- Assignment of duties
- Establishing reporting relation ship

➤ **Importance of organising**
- Benefits of specialisation
- Clarity in working relationships
- Optimum utilization of resources
- Adaption to change
- Effective administration
- Development of personnel
- Expansion and growth

➤ **Organisation Structure**
- Functional
- Divisional

➤ **Formal and Informal Organisation**

➤ **Delegations**
- **Elements**

(i) Authority
(ii) Responsibility
(iii) Accountability

- **Importance**

(i) Effective management
(ii) Employee Development
(iii) Motivation of Employees
(iv) Facilitation of growth
(v) Basis of Management hierarchy
(vi) Better Coordination

➤ **Centralisation and Decentralisation**
- **Importance**

(i) Develops initiative among subordinates
(ii) Develops managerial talents for the future
(iii) Quick decision making
(iv) Relief to top management
(v) Facilitates growth
(vi) Better control

MCQs

1. Which of the following points highlight the crucial role played by the organisation in any business enterprise?
   (a) Repetitive performance of a particular tasks leads to specialisation.
   (b) Hierarchical order structure is created which enables to fix the responsibility and extent of authority.
   (c) Clarity of working relationship enables proper execution of work.
   (d) All of above.
2. The management function which ensures that efforts are directed towards the attainment of goals as per the plans:
   (a) Directing (b) Staffing
   (c) Organising (d) Controlling
3. Which organisation structure provides benefits of occupational specialisation?
   (a) Functional (b) Divisional
   (c) Formal (d) Both a & b
4. Which one is not the step of organising process?
   (a) Departmentalisation
   (b) Assignment of duties
   (c) Standardisation
   (d) Establish relationship
5. The span of management gives shape to the organisational structure. It means:
   (a) It determines the number of departments in a firm.
   (b) Number of subordinate that can be effectively managed by a superior
   (c) Both (a) & (b) Above
   (d) None of the above.
6. Greater flexibility and initiative is found in which of the following organisational Structure:
   (a) Divisional structure
   (b) Functional Structure
   (c) Informal Structure
   (d) None of the above
7. Formal organisation does not provide a complete picture of how an organisation works. Which of the following statement does not highlight the above statement?
   (a) Does not provide adequate recognition to creative talent.
   (b) Procedural delays may be there
   (c) Too much emphasis on structure and work.
   (d) Fair predictability of behaviour of employees.
8. ____________ Is restricted by law, rules and regulations of the organisation:
   (a) Authority (b) Responsibility
   (c) Accountability (d) All of the above
9. Assertion (A) "For effective performance at work, there should be proper match between skills of the work force and competence."
   Reason (R) "The work must be assigned to those who are best fitted to perform it well".
   Choose:
   (a) Both (A) & (R) are true and (R) is the correct explanation of (A)
   (b) Both (A) & (R) are true and (R) is not correct explanation of (A)
   (c) (A) is true but (R) is false
   (d) (A) is false but (R) is true.
10. "Informal Organisation suffers from certain defects". Which of the following statement is not a defect of informal organisation:
   (a) Spreading rumours
   (b) There can be resistance to change causing delay in growth
   (c) Prescribed lines of communication is not followed

(d) It pressurises members to confirm to group expectations.

11. "Decentralisation is greatest when checking required on decisions taken by lower levels is least". This statement highlights one of the following:

(a) Quick decision making

(c) Relief to top management

(b) Better Control

(d) Facilitates growth

12. Statement I: 'Authority is delegation, responsibility is assumed and accountability is imposed'.

Statement II: 'Responsibility is derived from authority and accountability is derived from responsibility'.

(a) Both statement I & II are correct.

(b) Statement I is correct but II is incorrect.

(c) Statement I is incorrect and II is correct.

(d) Both Statement I & II are incorrect.

13. Every organisation must be characterised by both centralisation and decentralisation. This is required because:

(a) There is need for balance between these co-existing forces.

(b) Too much centralisation will obviate the need for management hierarchy.

(c) Too much decentralisation will obviate the need of higher Managerial positions.

(d) all of the above (a), (b), & (c).

14. A sound organisation structure will have the following benefits:

(a) Specialisation

(b) Classification of authority & Responsibility

(c) Avoiding duplication of work

(d) All of these.

15. Match the terms in Column I with suitable narration in Column II:

	Column I		Column II
I	Delegation	A.	Arises from formal position.
II	Decentralisation	B.	More control by superiors hence less freedom to take own decision.
III	Authority	C.	It an optional policy decision. It is done at the discretion of the top management.
IV	Responsibility	D.	Obligation to perform an assigned task.

Choose the right answer:

(a) I-B, II-D, III-A, IV-C

(b) I-D, II-C, III-B, IV-A

(c) I-B, II-C, III-A, IV-D

(d) I-C, II-D, III-A, IV-B

16. Which one of the mentioned below statement is not true for a formal organisation:

(a) Strict rules and regulations are followed in formal organisation.

(b) Psychological and social needs do not gets satisfied.

(c) It focusses on work only and ignores human relations.

(d) Formal organisation is dependent on informal organisation.

17. Establishing reporting relationship leads to:

(a) Identification and division of work

(b) Specialisation

(c) Better co-ordination amongst different departments.

(d) Decentralisation.

18. Which of the following statement is not true about elements of Delegation:

(a) Authority arises from the established scalars chain which links job positions .

(b) Authority relationships helps to maintain order in organisation

(c) Authority should be more than responsibility.

(d) Authority can be delegated but accountability cannot be.

19. Assertion (A): Departmentalisation establishes reporting relationship.

Reason (R): It creates hierarchical structure and helps in co-ordination between different departments.

(a) Both (A) & (R) are true and R is the correct explanation of A

(b) Both (A) & (R) are true and R is not the correct explanation of A

(c) A is true but R is false

(d) A is false but R is true

20. A pitfall of organising is that:

(a) Repetitive performance of the same job leads to monotony and boredom

(b) Specialisation of work.

(c) Division of work.

(d) Clarity in work relationship.

21. A flat structure of management has a

(a) Narrow span of management.

(b) Wide span of management.

(c) No span of management.

(d) Less levels of management.

22. Grouping of jobs of similar nature and organising these jobs as a separate department is part of:

(a) Decentralisation (b) Divisional

(c) Functional (d) Centralisation

23. A skilful manager uses the advantage of both formal and informal organisation so that the work continues smoothly. The points highlighted about informal organisation are

(a) Faster spread of information and quick feedback.

(b) Independent channel of Communication.

(c) The knowledge of such groups can be used to gather their support.

(d) all of above.

24. Arrange the following steps in process of organising in the correct sequence

(i) Assignment of duties

(ii) Departmentalisation

(iii) Identification and division of work

(iv) Establishing reporting relationship.

Choose the correct answer:

(a) (i), (ii), (iv) (iii) (b) (iii), (ii), (i), (iv)

(c) (iii), (ii), (iv), (i) (d) (ii), (iii), (i), (iv)

25. Match the term in Column I with most appropriate description in Column II:

	Column I		Column II
A.	Importance of organising	(i)	Activities are grouped on the basis of some criteria.
B.	Departmentalisation	(ii)	It leads to occupational specialisation
C.	Advantage of functional structure	(iii)	Conflicts may arise among different divisions.
D.	Disadvantage of Divisional Structure	(iv)	The proper assignment of jobs avoid overlapping of work and better utilisation of resources.

Choose the correct answer:

(a) A (iii), B (iv), C (i), D (ii)

(b) A (iv), B (i), C (ii), D (iii)

(c) A (ii), B (iii), C (iv), D (i)

(d) A (i), B (ii), C (iii), D (iv)

CHAPTER 6

Staffing

KEY POINTS

- **Meaning of Staffing**
  - "Putting people to jobs"
- **Right people for the right job**
  - Discovering and obtaining competent personnel for jobs
  - Ensures higher performance — putting right person on right job
  - Continuous survival and growth of the enterprise
  - Avoids overmanning, hence ensures optimum utilization of human resources
  - Improves job satisfaction and morale of employees
- **Staffing as a part of human resource management**
  - Recruitment
  - Job description
  - Compensation and incentive plans
  - Training and Development of employees
  - Maintaining labour relations
  - Handling grievances
  - Providing welfare of employees
  - Avoiding legal complications
- **Evolution of Human Resource Management**
- **Staffing Process**
  - Establishing the manpower requirement
  - Recruitment
  - Selection
  - Placement and orientation
  - Training and development
  - Performance appraisal
  - Promotion and career planning
  - Compensation
- **Recruitment & Sources**

Internal Sources

- Transfer
- Promotion

Merits & Demerits

External Sources

- Direct Recruitment
- Advertisements
- Placement Agencies
- Recommendation
- Advertising on TV
- Casual Callers
- Employment Exchange
- Campus Recruitment
- Labour Contractors
- Web Publishing

Merits & Demerits

- **Selection Process — Steps**
  - 1st Preliminary Screening
  - 2nd Selection Tests
    Intelligence Aptitude Personality Trade Interest test
  - 3rd Employment interview
  - 4th Reference and background check
  - 5th Selection decision
  - 6th Medical examination
  - 7th Job offer
  - 8th Contract of employment
- **Training and Development**
- **Importance and Benefits to Organisation**
  - Avoids wastage of efforts and money
  - Enhances employee productivity
  - Equips the future manager
  - Increases employee morale
  - Effective response to changing environment
- **Benefits to Employee**
  - Better career with improved skill
  - Better earning with increased performance
  - Less accidents
  - Increased satisfaction and morale of employees
- **Terms: Training, Education, Development**
- **Training Methods — Two Types**

  1st On the job
  - Apprenticeship programme
  - Coaching
  - Intern-ship training
  - Job rotation

  2nd Off the job
  - Classroom lectures / conferences
  - Films
  - Case study
  - Computer modelling
  - Vestibule training
  - Programmed Instruction

MCQs

1. The ability of an organisation to achieve its goal depends upon the quality of its human resources. Which of the following supports the above mentioned statement:
   (a) It ensures the continuous survival and growth of the enterprises.
   (b) Right person for the right job leads to higher performance.
   (c) It improves job satisfaction.
   (d) It helps in optimum utilisation of human resources.

2. Our assets walk out of the door each evening, we have to make sure they come back the next morning. This highlights the importance of which function of Management:
   (a) Staffing
   (b) Organising
   (c) Planning
   (d) Controlling

3. The long term success of a Company is usually examined on certain financial and non-financial parameter, One such non-financial parameter is:
   (a) Assets
   (b) Capital resources
   (c) Human resources
   (d) Creditors

4. Staffing is seen as a generic function of Management. It includes:
   (a) Training and Development of employee
   (b) Developing compensation and incentive plan
   (c) Handling grievances & complaints.
   (d) All of the above.

5. Staffing is referred to as both a line as well as a staff activity, which of the following are close to the above statement.
   (a) It is like other function of management like planning, organising, directing and controlling.
   (b) It is essential function of Manager and also has to play an advisory role.
   (c) It has a distinct functional area of Management like financial management.
   (d) It includes human relation department.

6. Which of the following is true for the Work Load Analysis:
   (a) Assessment of number and types of human resources necessary for performance of jobs and accomplishing the objective of the Firm.
   (b) It is analysis of number and types of workforce available to accomplish the jobs.
   (c) Analysing the difference between under staffing and over staffing.
   (d) All of the above.

7. Analysing existing employees is known as
   (a) Human resource management
   (b) Work force analysis
   (c) Job analysis
   (d) Work load analysis

8. Which of the following is not a step of staffing:
   (a) Recruitment
   (b) Selection
   (c) Standardisation
   (d) Training and Development

9. The process of searching for prospective employees and stimulating them to apply for jobs in called:
   (a) Promotion
   (b) Placement
   (c) Recruitment
   (d) Selection

10. Match the sources of recruitment in Column I with their nature of examples in Column II:

	Column I (Sources)		Column II
A.	Web publishing	(i)	Mainly for middle level and top level professional
B.	Management Consultancy	(ii)	www.naukri.com
C.	Campus recruitment	(iii)	Good source of skilled and unskilled operative jobs
D.	Employment exchange	(iv)	Fresh graduates can be moulded as per the requirement of the requirement of the company.

Choose the right answer:

(a) A (i), B. (iv), C (iii), D (ii)

(b) A (ii), B (i), C (iv), D (iii)

(c) A (ii), B (iv), C (iii), D (i)

(d) A (iv), B (ii), C(iii), D (i)

11. Internal sources of recruitment suffers from some defects, they are:

(a) Spirit of competition is hampered among employees.

(b) No scope of induction of fresh talent.

(c) Not suitable for new enterprise.

(d) It is very economical.

12. Senior Managers of Infosys Ltd. visit various professional colleges to get fresh graduates with latest technological know how – This method is called

(a) Direct recruitment

(b) Advertising

(c) Campus recruitment

(d) Labour contractors

13. People who provide the required number of unskilled workers at a short notice are called:-

(a) Jobbers

(b) Callers

(c) Employment Exchange

(d) Placement Agencies

14. The process of identifying and choosing the best person out of a number of prospective candidates for a job is called:

(a) Recruitment (b) Selection

(c) Development (d) Orientation

15. Which of the following is called a negative process:

(a) Recruitment (b) Development

(c) Training (d) Selection

16. Match the meaning of concepts in column I with concepts of staffing in column II:

	Column I		Column II
A.	It is the process of identifying and choosing the most eligible one.	(i)	Recruitment
B.	Searching for the prospective candidates.	(ii)	Job Analysis
C.	Defining all content, authority and responsibility relating to the job	(iii)	Job specification
D.	Qualification, attributes which a person must possess to apply for a job.	(iv)	Selection

Choose the right answer:

(a) A (iv), B (i), C (ii), D (iii)

(b) A (iii), B (ii), C (i), D (iv)

(c) A (i), B (iv), C (iii), D (ii)

(d) A (iv), B (ii), C (iii), D (i)

17. The process of familiarisation of employee is crucial and has a lasting impact. This step is:

(a) Selection (b) Training

(c) Orientation (d) Promotion

Read the text and answer questions 18 and 19

18. Mr. Abhay Sharma has joined a manufacturing company as a CEO of the company. His terms of compensation included Salary + HRA +

Incentives on sales + 5% Commission on profits + Vacations + Club membership + medical benefits.

Which of these items are indirect payments:

(a) Incentives & Commission
(b) Vacation + Club membership + medical benefits
(c) Commission + vacation
(d) HRS + commission +salary

19. Mr. Abhay's terms of compensation can be said to be on the basis of:

(a) Time
(b) Performance
(c) Combination of time and performance
(d) None of the above

20. The candidate who has applied for the job, can get this queries clarified during which of the following steps of selection procedure:

(a) Tests
(b) Employment interviews
(c) Medical Examination
(d) Selection

21. A document which contains vital details about the candidate, which is also authenticated and attested by him is called:

(a) Job offer
(b) Contract of Employment
(c) Medical fitness certificate
(d) Application form

22. The focus of ________ is to develop logical and rational mind while the focus of ________ is to improve work efficiency.

Choose the right answer:

(a) Education, Training
(b) Development, Education
(c) Training, Development
(d) Training, Education

23. The selection of candidate involves series of steps. Arrange them in correct order:

I. Employment Interview
II. Job offer
III. Checking the references
IV. Selection Tests

Choose the correct answer:

(a) (iv), (i), (iii), (ii) (b) (ii), (iv), (iii), (i)
(c) (iii),(iv), (ii), (i) (d) (iii), (ii), (i), (iv)

24. When employees are required to handle sophisticated machinery & equipments, they are given:

(a) Classroom lectures
(b) Programmed Instruction
(c) Vestibule Training
(d) Computer modelling

25. This type of training makes the employees ready for replacement or transfer or promotion:

(a) Job rotation
(b) Vestibule
(c) Apprenticeship Programme
(d) Programmed Instruction

26. Under which method of training a trainee works under the guidance of master worker:

(a) Apprenticeship Program
(b) Internship
(c) Vestibule
(d) Induction

27. The concept which involves the growth of employee in all respect is:

(a) Training
(b) Promotion
(c) Transfer
(d) Development

28. Internal source of Recruitment are considered to be more economical because:-

(a) No money needs to be on advertisement
(b) Very less training is required to existing staff
(c) Very less turnover as rules & regulations are known
(d) All of the above

29. Match the Type of test in Column I with Purpose in Column II:

Column I		Column II	
A.	Personality Test	(i)	Ability to make decision and judgement
B.	Trade Test	(ii)	To judge the potential of the candidate to learn the new skills
C.	Intelligence Test	(iii)	To know the emotional reactions, maturity and value system.
D.	Aptitude Test	(iv)	To test the level of knowledge and proficiency in the area of profession.

Choose the correct answer:

(a) A (ii), B (i), C (iv), D (iii)
(b) A (iii), B (iv), C (i), D (ii)
(c) A (i), B (ii), C (iii), D (iv)
(d) A (iv), B (iii), C (ii), D (i)

30. Human Resource Management in its present form has involved a number of significant inter related developments. They are:

(a) Industrial Revolution
(b) Emergence of trade union movement
(c) Factory System
(d) All of the above

31. Certain workforce in a factory are unable to learn and understand the working of a new machine. As a result they constantly refer to their supervisor to help them. This leads to lot of wastage of time of the supervisor and also resources of the company. The Supervisor decided to give them some training. Which one of the following is most suitable in the above case:

(a) On the job training (b) Off the job training
(c) Orientation training (d) Vestibule training

32. As a line manager of a small organisation, Raju has to perform all functions of management. What are the additional steps in staffing process he has to undertake:

(a) Performance appraisal
(b) Career Planning
(c) Compensation
(d) All of the above

33. Match the tests that must be conducted as a part of selection procedure for the following jobs:

Match the following:

Column I		Column II	
A.	Security Officer	(i)	Interest Test
B.	Computer Operator	(ii)	Intelligence Test
C.	A Fashion Designer	(iii)	Trade Test
D.	College Lectures	(iv)	Personality Test

Choose the correct answer:

(a) A (ii), B (iii), C (i), D (iv)
(b) A (iv), B (iii), C (i), D (ii)
(c) A (iv), B (ii), C (i), D (iii)
(d) A (iii), B (ii), C (i), D (iv)

CHAPTER 7

Directing

KEY POINTS

- **Meaning and Characteristics**
  - Initiates action
  - At every level of management
  - Continuous process
  - Flows from top to bottom
- **Importance of Directing**
  - Initiates action which leads to attainment of desired objectives
  - Integrates employees efforts which contributes to organisational performance
  - Motivation and effective leadership
  - Facilitates introduction of needed change in the organisation
  - Brings stability and balance in the organisation
- **Principles of Directing**
  - Maximum individual contribution
  - Harmony of objectives
  - Unity of command
  - Appropriate direction technique
  - Managerial communication
  - Use of informal organisation
  - Leadership
  - Follow through
- **Elements of Direction**
  - **Supervision**

(i) Maintains relations with workers as a guide, friend and philosopher

(ii) Link between worker and management

(iii) Maintains group unity among workers

(iv) Takes responsibility of task achievement

(v) Provides good 'On the job' training

(vi) Builds morale among workers by his good leadership

(vii) Provides feedback of work done by analysing it

- **Motivation**
  - Motive, Motivation, Motivator

(i) It is an internal feeling

(ii) It produces goal directed behaviour

(iii) It is either positive or negative

(iv) It is complex process

- **Motivation process**
  - **Importance**

(i) Improvement of performance levels of employees

(ii) Helps to change negative to positive attitudes of employees

(iii) Reduces employee turnover and absenteeism

(iv) Bring out changes without much resistance in an orginisation

- **Maslow Need Hierarchy Theory**
- **Financial Incentives**
  - Pay and allowances
  - Productivity linked wage incentives
  - Bonus

- Profit sharing
- Stock option
- Retirement benefits
- Perquisites

➤ **Non-financial Incentives**

- Status
- Organisational Climate
- Career Advancement Opportunity
- Job Enrichment
- Employee recognition programme
- Job security
- Employee participation
- Employee empowerment

➤ **Leadership**

- Ability to influence others
- Bring change in behaviour of others
- Interpersonal relations between leaders and followers
- Exercised to achieve common organisational goals
- Continuous process

➤ **Qualities : Style**

- Autocratic
- Democratic
- Laissez-faire

➤ **Communication**

- **Elements of communication process**

(i) Sender

(ii) Message

(iii) Encoding

(iv) Media

(v) Decoding

(vi) Receiver

(vii) Feedback

(viii) Noise

- **Importance**

(i) Formal

(ii) Informal

➤ **Barriers to communication**

- Semantic
- Psychological
- Organisational
- Personal

➤ **Improving communication effectiveness**

- Clarity of ideas before communication
- Communication according to the need of receiver
- Consult others before communicating
- Be aware of languages, tone and content of message
- Proper feedback
- Convey things of help and value to listeners
- Communication for the present as well as future
- Follow up communications
- Be a good listener
- Completeness of message

MCQs

1. "Hands off" leadership style relates to:
   (a) Participative (b) Autocratic
   (c) Laissez - faire (d) None of the above

2. Which of the following is a financial incentive:
   (a) Employee participation
   (b) Promotion
   (c) Job Security
   (d) Stock Option

3. Which function of Management initiates action in an organisation:
   (a) Organising (b) Directing
   (c) Staffing (d) Controlling

4. Directing is not mere issue of communication but also other things such as:
   (a) Supervision (b) Motivation
   (c) Leadership (d) All of above

5. 'A good leader identifies the potential of his employees and encourages them to extract work up to their full potential.' The element of Directing' highlighted here is:
   (a) Motivation (b) Leadership
   (c) Supervision (d) Communication

6. Providing effective directing is a challenging task. Which of these principles do not assist in directing process.
   (a) Harmony of objective
   (b) Appropriate use of direction
   (c) External inputs
   (d) Unity of Command

7. Directing is performed at
   (a) Top level (b) Middle level
   (c) Supervisory level (d) All levels

8. (1) _________ stimulates people to action to accomplish goals.
   (2) _________ is a inner state that directs behaviour towards goals.
   (3) _________ is a technique used influence people in organisation to do their best.

   Choose the right answer to fill up the blanks above:
   (a) Motive, Motivation, Motivator
   (b) Motivation, Motive, Motivator
   (c) Motivator, Motivation, Motive
   (d) Motive, Motivator, Motivation

9. Abraham Maslow, known for his Need hierarchy theory was a
   (a) Sociologist
   (b) Psychologist
   (c) Management Scientist
   (d) Geologist

10. Arrange the following needs of an employee working in an organisation on the basis of Maslow's Need Hierarchy Theory.
    (A) Job Title
    (B) Achievement of goal
    (C) Basic Salary
    (D) Affiliation
    (E) Pension Plan

    Choose the correct answer:
    (a) B, C, E, A, D (b) A, D, C, E, B
    (c) B, C, D, A, E (d) C, E, D, A, B

Read the text and solve the question.

M/s AIFA LTD are dealing in Manufacturing of small electrical gadgets. The firm has three departments. Each headed by a supervisor. The Departments are ***Electric Iron, Lighting & Switches.***

It was noticed that many cases of employees' misbehaviour discontentment and even labour turnover were coming from ***Electric Iron department***. The supervisor of this department was short tempered and dictatorial.

The Manager of the firm sent an expert to find out the root cause of this problem. The expert was advised to make judgement through informal communications. After analysing, the expert gave his report and certain steps, if implemented well, could solve the problem.

11. Which element of directing function is missing in M/s Alfa Ltd:

(a) Motivation (b) Communication

(c) Supervision (d) Leadership

12. Which are the steps that should be taken to solve the problems of this department:

(a) Improve the working conditions.

(b) Adequate reward and recognition is given to the deserving employee.

(c) Supervisor is guided to show better behaviour and friendly relations with workers.

(d) All of the above.

13. The supervisor of Dept. Electric Iron followed which leadership style:

(a) Laissez faire (b) Authoritarian

(c) Democratic (d) None of the above

14. The Manager asked the expert to follow the informal communication, which of the following is the advantage of informal communication:

(a) It follows no formal lines of communication

(b) The employees exchange their views which cannot be done through formal channels.

(c) The source of information is not easily tracked, so can be misleading.

(d) It spreads fast and have chances of getting distorted.

15. Which of this is concerned with designing jobs that include greater variety of work content:

(a) Promotion

(b) Career advancement

(c) Job Enrichment

(d) Employee Recognition programme

16. Which of the following is non-financial incentives:

(a) Ranking or position in organisation

(b) Career advancement

(c) Job enrichment

(d) All of above.

17. Directing abilities of a manager mainly depends upon his ________ skill, without which his knowledge and intelligence has no meaning.

(a) Leadership (b) Motivation

(c) Supervision (d) Communication

18. The process of converting the message into communication symbols is known as

(a) Media (b) Encoding

(c) Feedback (d) Decoding

19. The Communication network in which all subordinates under a supervisor communicate through the supervisor only is:

(a) Single chain (b) Inverted "V"

(c) Wheel (d) Circular

20. The communication gap due to size and complexity of organisation structure comes under the following category:

(a) Psychological barrier

(b) Personal barrier

(c) Sematic barrier

(d) Organisational barrier

21. Use of "Technical jargons" is which type of communication barrier:

(a) Organisational (b) Sematic

(c) Psychological (d) Personal

22. Match the "Barrier of Communication" in Column I with their examples in Column II:

	Column –I		Column –II
1	Sematic Barrier	(i)	Status of Superior
2	Psychological Barrier	(ii)	Lack of proper incentives
3	Organisational Barrier	(iii)	Faulty translation of Message
4	Personal Barrier	(iv)	Premature Evaluation

Choose the answer:

(a) 1 (ii), 2 (iii), 3 (iv), 4 (i)

(b) 1 (iii), 2 (iv), 3 (i), 4 (ii)

(c) 1 (iv), 2 (ii), 3 (iii), 4 (i)

(d) 1 (i), 2 (ii), 3 (iv), 4 (iii)

Read the text and solve the question:

Rajan who works in a popular coffee house, gets selected for the`Best Employee of the month'.

His name and photograph is placed on the notice board of the café. He is also given a batch to wear stating `Best Employee for that particular month'.

23. In the narration above, giving such incentives are called:

(a) Job Enrichment

(b) Career Advancement opportunity

(c) Employee recognition programme

(d) Employee participation

24. Raghu joined a government job after serving in a private company for 8 years. One of the reason he mentioned were the retirement benefits his new job offered. Which of this highlights retirement benefits:

(a) Medical aid

(b) Pension and gratuity

(c) Dearness allowance

(d) Increments.

25. Which of the following is not an element of communication process:

(a) Decoding (b) Communication

(c) Channel (d) Media

26. To get the real feedback of employees the manager must make use of:

(a) Formal Communication

(b) Informal Communication

(c) Both a) & b)

(d) None of the above

27. Match the Elements of directing in Column-I with their correct meaning in Column-II:

	Column-I		Column-II
A.	Motivation	(1)	The process of watching the employees performing the job.
B.	Communication	(2)	It is activity of influencing people to strive willingly for group objectives.
C.	Supervision	(3)	It is two way process It starts with a sender and ends with a sender.
D.	Leadership	(4)	It is the process which propels people to action and continuous them in action to the best of their ability.

Choose the correct answer:

(a) A (4), B (3), C (1), D (2)

(b) A (1), B (2), C (4), D (3)

(c) A (4), B (2), C (1), D (4)

(d) A (1), B (4), C (3), D (2)

28. Which of these statements highlights the role of proper feedback in improving communication effectiveness:

(a) The receiver of communication may also be encouraged to respond to the message

(b) It helps in removing hurdles in implementing.

(c) The language used should be understandable.

(d) Subordinates should be clear in all its perspective.

29. Under this style of leadership, the leader takes decisions in consultation and participation with employees. This type of leadership style is called

(a) Autocratic (b) Democratic

(c) Free - rein (d) None of the above

30. "Directing takes place wherever Superior Subordinate relations exist." Identify the characteristics highlighted in the above statement.

(a) Directing initiates action

(b) Directing is continuous process

(c) Directing flows from top to bottom

(d) Directing takes place at all levels.

CHAPTER 8

Controlling

KEY POINTS

- **Meaning of Controlling Function**
  - All pervasive
- **Importance of Controlling**
  - Accomplishing organisational goals
  - Judging accuracy of standards
  - Making efficient use of resources
  - Improving employee motivation
  - Ensuring order and discipline
  - Facilitating coordination in action
- **Limitations of Controlling**
  - Difficulty in setting quantitative standards
  - Little control on external factors
  - Resistance from employees
  - Costly affair
- **Relationship between Planning & Controlling**
  - Planning is prescriptive whereas controlling is evaluative.
- **Controlling Process Setting**
  - 1st Step – Performance Standard
  - 2nd Step – Measurement of Actual Performance
  - 3rd Step – Comparing Actual Performance with Standards
  - 4th Step – Analysing Deviation

    ↓ Critical Point Control ↓ Management by Exception
  - 5th Step – Taking Corrective Actions

MCQs

1. Which function brings the management cycle back to planning function.
   (a) Organising (b) Staffing
   (c) Directing (d) Controlling
2. "Planning is prescriptive whereas controlling is evaluative". Which of the following is highlighted here:
   (a) Planning and controlling are interdependent and inter related activities.
   (b) They are forward looking and backward looking.
   (c) Both of the above points
   (d) None of the above points.
3. Controlling is
   (a) Backward looking function.
   (b) Forward looking function.
   (c) Both backward looking and forward looking function.
   (d) None of the above.
4. Labour unions are objecting to the introduction of CCTV (closed circuit television) in a modern tea factory. Which function of management will help in overcoming this issue.
   (a) Staffing function
   (b) Directing function
   (c) Controlling function
   (d) Organising function
5. Which of the following is not an 'importance of controlling function'?
   (a) It helps in judging accuracy of standards.
   (b) It improves employees motivation.
   (c) It helps in accomplishing the organisation goals.
   (d) It restricts coordination in action.
6. Controlling is a systematic process involving various steps. Which of the following is not a step in the process of controlling.
   (a) Analysing deviations
   (b) Establishing reporting relationship
   (c) Setting standards
   (d) Taking corrective actions.
7. Performance standards can be set in the following terms:
   (a) Qualitative
   (b) Quantitative
   (c) Both Qualitative & Quantitative
   (d) Neither Qualitative nor Quantitative
8. A Manager who tries to control everything ends up controlling nothing. This highlights the principle of
   (a) Span of Control
   (b) Management by exception
   (c) Delegation of Authority
   (d) Unity of Command
9. If the deviations are below the permissible limit in a controlling process, what action should be taken:
   (a) To be reported at top level
   (b) Should be ignored
   (c) Corrective action to be taken
   (d) None of the above
10. Assertion (A): Controlling function of a Manager is a pervasive function .

    Reason (R): Controlling is as much required in an educational institution, Defence Forces, Hospital and a club as in any business organisation .
    (a) Both (A) and (R) are true and (R) is the correct explanation of (A)
    (b) Both (A) and (R) are true but (R) is not the correct explanation of (A)
    (c) (A) is true but (R) is false
    (d) (A) is false but (R) is true
11. Last step of controlling process is
    (a) Setting standard
    (b) Taking corrective action
    (c) Measuring actual performance
    (d) Qualifying deviation.

12. Deviations in controlling process means difference between standard performance and

(a) Actual performance

(b) Future performance

(c) Both of the above points

(d) None of the above

13. Control should focus on key results area which are __________ to the success of an Organisation.

(a) Critical (b) Involved

(c) Flexible (d) Consistent

14. Ramesh Kumar a Manager of a firm wants to fix standard of production of worker in precise quantitative terms. Under which function of Management this can be done:

(a) Controlling (b) Planning

(c) Directing (d) Organising

15. With the help of controlling function , the Management can know not only about the deficiency In the performance but it also helps Management to know whether standards or plans are set correctly or not. The importance of Management discussed above is

(a) Ensuring order and discipline

(b) Judging accuracy of standard

(c) Making efficient use of resources

(d) Facilitating co-ordination in action.

CHAPTER 9

Financial Management

KEY POINTS

- **Meaning of Finance**
- **Meaning of Financial Management**
- **Role of Financial Management**
  - Size and Composition of Fixed Assets
  - Quantum to Current Assets and its breakup into cash, inventory
  - Long term & Short Term Funds available
  - Breakup of Long term Financing into debt, equity etc.
  - All items in P&L etc.
- **Objectives** – Wealth maximization concept
- **Financial Decisions**
- **Investment Decision**
- **Factors Affecting Capital Budgeting Decisions:**
  - Cash flow of the project
  - Rate of Return
  - Investment criteria involved
- **Factors affecting Financing Decision:**
  - Cost
  - Fixed Operating Cost
  - Risk
  - Cashflow position of the company
  - Floatation Cost
  - Control Considerations
  - State of Capital Market
- **Factors affecting Dividend Decision:**
  - Amount of Earnings
  - Stability Earnings
  - Stability Dividends
  - Growth Opportunities
  - Cash Flow Position
  - Shareholders Preference
  - Taxation Policy
  - Stock Market Reaction
  - Access to Capital Market
  - Legal Constraints
  - Contractual Constraints
- **Financial Planning Objective**
  - Availability of Fund when Required
  - Funds are not raised unnecessarily
- **Importance of Financial Planning**
  - Helps in forecasting
  - Better preparedness for future
  - Coordinating business functions
  - Avoidance of wastage
  - Link of present with future
  - Link between investment and financing decisions
  - Makes evaluation of actual performance easy
- **Capital Structure**

- **Factors Determining Choice of Capital Structure**
  - Cash Flow Position
  - Interest Coverage Ratio = $\frac{\text{EBIT}}{\text{Interest}}$
  - Debt Service Coverage Ratio $= \frac{\text{PATID + Non Cash Exp.}}{\text{Preference Divid + Interest + Repayment}}$
  - Return on Investment – Trading on Equity
  - Cost of Debt
  - Tax Rate
  - Cost of Equity
  - Floatation Cost
  - Risk Consideration
  - Flexibility
  - Regulatory Framework
  - Stock Market Conditions
  - Control
  - Capital Structure of other companies
- **Management of Fixed Capital**
  - **Factors affecting requirement of Fixed Capital**

(i) Nature of Business

(ii) Scale of Operations

(iii) Choice of Technique

(iv) Technology Up-gradation

(v) Growth Prospects

(vi) Diversification

(vii) Financing Alternatives

(viii) Level of Collaboration

- **Working Capital Meaning**
  - **Factors Affecting Working Capital Requirements**

(i) Nature of business

(ii) Scale of operations

(iii) Business Cycle

(iv) Seasonal factors

(v) Production Cycle

(vi) Credit Allowed

(vii) Credit Availed

(viii) Operating Efficiency

(ix) Availability of raw Material

(x) Growth Prospects

(xi) Level of Competition

(xii) Inflation

MCQs

1. "The overall financial health of a business is determined by the quality of its Financial Management". Which of the following highlights the role of Financial Management:
   (a) The amount of long term and short term funds to be used.
   (b) Amount and composition of current assets.
   (c) Breaking-up of long term financing in debt and equity etc.
   (d) All of above.

2. The primary aim of financial management is best known by ____________ concept.
   (a) Wealth Maximization
   (b) Cost Minimization
   (c) Investment Maximization
   (d) Profit Maximisation.

3. The Decisions regarding from where and when to purchase funds is
   (a) Financial Decision (b) Dividend decision
   (c) Investment Decision (d) None of the above

4. Which of the following is not a factor affecting the financing decision of a firm:
   (a) Cost of raising funds.
   (b) Risk associated with source of fund.
   (c) Control Consideration.
   (d) Stock Market operations.

5. The decision in financial management which determines the proportion between Debt and Equity Funds is called
   (a) Financing decision
   (b) Investment decision
   (c) Capital Structure
   (d) Dividend decision

6. Match the following concepts in Column-A with their example and meaning in Column-B:

	Column-A		Column-B
A.	Capital Budgeting	1.	Owners funds and borrowed fund
B.	Financial leverage	2.	Purchase of fixed asset
C.	Capital Structure	3.	The proportion of debt in the overall capital
D.	Working Capital decisions	4.	levels of inventory and receivable

   Choose the correct answer:
   (a) A-2, B-3, C-1, D-4 (b) A-4, B-2, C-3, D-1
   (c) A-1, B-4, C-2, D-3 (d) A-3, B-2, C-4, D-1

7. When the tax rates are low, a company can declare ______________ dividends.
   (a) higher (b) lower
   (c) No dividend (d) Stabilised dividend

8. Which one of the following is not a factor affecting dividend decisions of a firm.
   (a) Amount of earnings of the firm
   (b) Stability of earning
   (c) Free legal policy
   (d) Shareholders preferences

9. Contractual constraints as a factor affecting Dividend decisions means:
   (a) Dividend should be paid only as mentioned in a contract.
   (b) Loan agreements may show restrictions on dividend payment by financier.
   (c) This applies only in short term loan.
   (d) None of above.

10. The importance of financial planning can best be described as:
   (a) Acts as link between Investing and financial decisions.
   (b) Reduction of wastages & duplication.

(c) Clear policies & procedures.

(d) All of above.

11. Big companies and financial institutions prefer to invest in a company with regular and stable dividend policy. This means dividend is increased only when

(a) Earning potential has gone up

(b) Earning of current year alone is not the criteria for increased dividend.

(c) Both (a) & (b) above

(d) None of the above

12. The size of assets, the profitability and competitiveness are all affected by ______

(a) Investment decision (b) Dividend decision

(c) Financing decision (d) Capital Budgeting

13. Growth opportunities affect Dividend decisions because:

(a) It affects cash flow position

(b) Firms retain earnings more and declare less dividend

(c) Dividends are paid out of current and past earnings

(d) None of the above

14. Determination of total capital requirement is vital in financial planning. for this Finance Manager has to find future prospects by forecasting of ______

(a) Stock Market (b) Sales

(c) Consumers (d) Competitors

15. Higher Debt/ Equity ratio results in

(a) Lower financial risks

(b) Higher degree of operating risks

(c) Higher degree of financial risks

(d) Higher EPS

16. Assertion (A) "Debt is cheaper but is more risky for a business"

Reason (R) Payment of Interest and repayment of principal is obligatory for the business

(a) Both (A) and (R) are true, (R) is the correct explanation of (A)

(b) Both (A) & (R) are true but (R) is not the correct explanation of (A)

(c) (A) is true but (R) is false

(d) (A) is false but (R) is true.

17. Kinder Home space' started an online business to sell Bed linens, fitted bed sheet sets. They knew that there were other sellers too in their product market. Identify the important factor which would affect their working capital requirements:

(a) Seasonal factors

(b) Level of competition

(c) Production cycle

(d) Growth prospects

18. During depression in market, which source of fund is advised to the Company to raise fund:

(a) Debt (b) Equity

(c) Debt + Equity (d) None of the above

19. If there are large number of retired and middle class shareholders who prefer regular income, then the firm should prefer giving ______

(a) Low dividend (b) High dividend

(c) No dividend (d) Stable dividend

20. What are the factors affecting investing decisions.

(a) Return on Investment

(b) Stability of dividends

(c) Floatation cost

(d) Earning

21. Stock market condition is a factor related to:

(a) Financing decision

(b) Dividend decision

(c) Financial planning

(d) Investment decision

22. The cost of raising funds is called:

(a) Fixed cost (b) Floatation cost

(c) Marginal cost (d) Variable cost

23. Working capital requirement and operating cycle have a link. Choose the correct option:
   (a) Longer the operating cycle, more is requirement of working capital.
   (b) Longer the operating cycle lesser the working capital requirement.
   (c) Operating cycle and working capital requirement have no link.
   (d) Shorter the operating cycle more is requirement of working capital.

Read the text and answer the question:

Mr. Ranbir is the owner of 'Ranbir sports club' having facility for different sports including football. Till now the company had been operating on owners' funds. Keeping in view of his plan to set up one more club, exclusive for football, in a different part of the city, the company raised debt capital to take advantage of trading on equity. The proportion of debt in the total capital of the company is 30% .the debt has been raised @ 12% whereas the return on investment is 10%, However, even after employing debt, the EPS' of the company is falling.

24. The factor which favoured the issue of debt by the company:
   (a) No flotation cost
   (b) Risk consideration
   (c) Stock market condition
   (d) Capital structure of other companies.

25. The EPS of the firm is declining even after utilising debt, This is because_________
   (a) ROI should be higher than the rate of interest.
   (b) ROI should be same as rate of interest
   (c) ROI and rate of interest are not affecting each other.
   (d) None of the above.

26. The objective of Mr. Ranbir was to have a judicious mix of Owners' fund and Debt. The Proportion of Debt in overall capital is called __________
   (a) Capital structure (b) Financial leverage
   (c) Equity Trading (d) None of the above.

27. Current assets of a business firm should be financed through:
   (a) Current liability only
   (b) Long term liability only
   (c) Partly from both current liability & long term liability
   (d) None of the above.

28. Net working capital may be defined as
   (a) Excess of current assets over current liabilities.
   (b) Excess of current liabilities over current asset
   (c) Both of the above (a) & (b)
   (d) None of the above.

29. Fixed capital is financed through which of the following sources of fund:
   (a) Debentures (b) Equity shares
   (c) Preference shares (d) All of these.

30. A company's earnings before interest and tax is Rs.25 lakhs. It pays 10% interest on its debts. His total investment is Rs. 1 crore. Calculate the company's ROI.
   (a) 20% (b) 25%
   (c) 10% (d) 30%

31. If the company wants to raise capital by Debt or Equity, your advise with reason will be:
   (a) Debt because ROI > Rate of Interest
   (b) Debt because raising fund as debt is gainful for equity shareholder
   (c) Debt because concept applied here is trading on equity.
   (d) All of the above.

CHAPTER 10

Financial Market

KEY POINTS

- **Sensex – launched on 1986**
- **Concept of Financial Market**
- **Functions of Financial Market**
  - Mobilisation of saving and channeling them into productive use
  - Facilitating price discovery
  - Providing liquidility to financial assets
  - Reducing the cost of transactions
- **Classification of Financial Market (FM)**

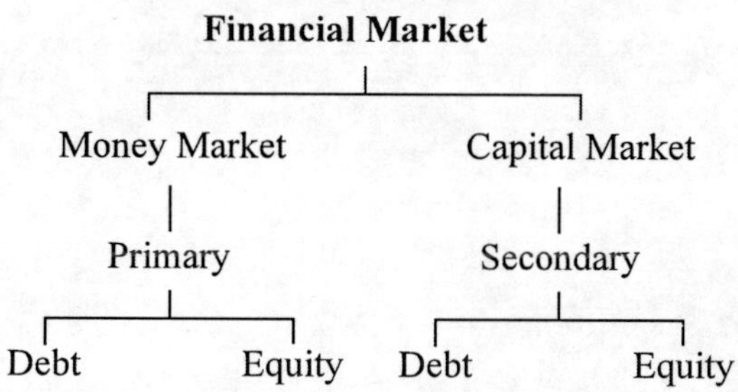

- **Money Market Instruments**
  - Treasury Bill
  - Commercial Paper
  - Call Money
  - Certificate of Deposit
  - Commercial Bill
- **Distinction between Capital Market and Money Market**
  - Participants
  - Instruments
  - Investment Outlay
  - Duration
  - Liquidity
  - Safety
  - Expected return
- **Primary Market**
- **Methods of Floatation of new issue**
  - Offer through prospectus
  - Offer for sale
  - Private Placement
  - Rights Issue
  - E-IPOs
- **Secondary Market**
- **Stock Exchange – Meaning & Functions**
  - Providing Liquidity and Market ability to existing securities
  - Pricing of Securities
  - Safety of Transaction
  - Contribution to Economic growth
  - Spreading of Equity Cult
  - Providing scope for speculation
- **Trading and Settlement Procedure**
- **Advantages of Electronic or Screen based trading**
  - Ensures transparency
  - One Trading Platform
  - Increases efficiency of operations so helps in fixing prices
  - Reduction in time, cost and risk of errors

- Enabled a large number of participants to trade with each other thereby improving the liquidity of the market

➤ **Steps in trading and settlement procedure**

➤ **De materialisation and Depositories**

➤ **NSDL and CDSL**

➤ **National Stock Exchange of India (NSE)**

➤ **BSE**

➤ **SEBI – purpose, role, objective and functions of SEBI**

Functions of SEBI

- Regulatory Function
- Development Function
- Protective Function

➤ **Organisation Structure of SEBI**

MCQs

1. In financial market, instruments with maturity of less than one year is Traded in
   (a) Money Market (b) Capital Market
   (c) Primary Market (d) Industrial Market

2. Allocative function of financial market is
   (a) Linking the savers and investors
   (b) Enabling savers to invest their surplus funds
   (c) Enables the investors to borrow funds as per their requirement.
   (d) All of above.

3. Funds which are raised through commercial paper and used for seasonal and working capital needs is known as
   (a) Call Money
   (b) Certificate of deposit
   (c) Bridge financing
   (d) None of above

4. Call Money, commercial paper, certificate of deposits are instrument of
   (a) Capital Market
   (b) Money Market
   (c) Both (a) & (b) above
   (d) None of above

5. Commercial paper is short term, unsecured promissory note having a maturity period of
   (a) 15 days to one year (b) 2 days
   (c) 180 days (d) 91 days to one year

6. Treasury bill are issued in the form of promissory note for a minimum amount of ___
   (a) Rs. 2500 (b) Rs. 25000
   (c) Rs. 1000 (d) Rs. 10000

7. Match the following Money Market Instruments in Column-I with the terms connected in Column-II:

	Column-I		Column-II
A.	Commercial paper	(i)	Zero Coupon Bond
B.	Commercial Bill	(ii)	Bridge financing
C.	Call Money	(iii)	Trade Bill
D.	Treasury Bill	(iv)	Inter Bank Money Market

Choose the correct answer:
   (a) A - (ii) B - (iii) C - (i) D - (iv)
   (b) A - (ii) B - (iii) C - (iv) D - (i)
   (c) A - (iv) B - (i) C - (iii) D - (ii)
   (d) A - (i) B - (ii) C - (iii) D - (iv)

8. Which money market instrument can be issued to individuals, corporations and companies during period of tight liquidity when deposit growth of bank is slow but demand of credit is high.
   (a) Treasury bill
   (b) Call Money
   (c) Commercial bill
   (d) Certificate of deposit

9. 'Odd lot trading' means trading in multiples of
   (a) 100 stock or less (b) 10 stock or less
   (c) 50 stock or less (d) None of above

10. A Ideal capital market is one where:
    (a) Finance is available at reasonable cost
    (b) Market operations are free & fair, competitive and transparent
    (c) Capital market allocates capital most productively
    (d) All of above

11. To meet floatation costs, firm generally issue the following instruments of money market:
    (a) Treasury Bill (b) Commercial paper
    (c) Commercial bill (d) Call money

12. The duration of Money Market instrument is maximum

(a) One year (b) two years

(c) 90 days (d) 180 days

13. Which of the following are not instruments traded in Capital Market

(a) Shares (b) Debentures

(c) Commercial papers (d) Preference Shares.

14. DFHI has been established for the specific objective of providing a ready market for Money Market instruments. What does DFHI stand for:

(a) Deposit financial head of India

(b) Discount finance head of India

(c) Depository funding head of India

(d) None of the above

15. Treasury Bills are issued by

(a) Government of India

(b) RBI

(c) Companies

(d) None of above

16. Trading of existing securities is done in ________

(a) Primary Market (b) Secondary Market

(c) Both (a) & (b) (d) None of above

17. The existing share holders are offered right to buy new shares of a company is called ________

(a) e - IPOs (b) Right issue

(c) Private placement (d) None of above

18. Which of the following are the functions of Stock Exchange:

(a) Providing liquidity and marketability to existing securities

(b) Spreading a Equity Cult

(c) Providing scope for healthy speculation

(d) All of above

19. The apex body who controls the capital market of our country is:

(a) RBI (b) SEBI

(c) SBI (d) None of above

20. A note counting the details of number of shares bought/sold, price and other details is called___

(a) Depository (b) Credit Note

(c) Contract note (d) Deposit note

21. Rearrange correctly the trading procedure on a stock exchange.

(a) Placing the order

(b) Match the share and best price

(c) Issue of contract Note

(d) Delivery of share and its payment

(e) Opening of Demat account with depository

(f) Execute the order

Choose the correct answer:

(a) e a b f c d (b) d b c e f a

(c) a b e c d f (d) a e b c f d

22. Depository participants are:-

(a) The intermediaries who serve as link between investors and depository.

(b) The intermediaries who serve as link between one investors and company .

(c) Both a & b above

(d) None of the above.

23. Screen based trading is called

(a) Electronic trading system

(b) Private placement

(c) Indirect trading

(d) None of the above.

24. Which of the following parties are permitted to become Depository participant's

(a) Clearing Corporations

(b) Stock brokers

(c) Financial Institutions

(d) All of the above.

25. Assertion (A) Stock Exchange have played a vital role in spreading of Equity cult.

Reason (R) Stock exchanges have taken effective steps in educating the public about investment following better trading practises and regulating new issue.

(a) Both assertion (A) and reason (R) are true and (R) is the correct explanation of (A)
(b) Both (A) and (R) are true and (R) is not the correct explanation of A.
(c) A is true but R is false
(d) A is false but R is true.

26. The settlement cycle in NSE called pay-out day is done in
(a) T + 1 (b) T + 2
(c) T + 3 (d) T + 4

27. The National stock exchange started with trading on wholesale debt market segment in the Year.
(a) 1993 (b) 1994
(c) 2000 (d) 1992

28. SEBI was given statutory status as a body corporate on:
(a) April' 1988 (b) Jan' 1992
(c) May' 1992 (d) None of the above.

29. _______________ is a technology driven electronic storage system promoted by NSE
(a) CDSL (b) NSDL
(c) SBI (d) NYSE

30. Electronic holding of shares is called
(a) Rematerialisation
(b) Dematerialisation
(c) Both (a) & (b)
(d) None of the above

31. Training of intermediaries of the securities market is a function of SEBI. It can be clarified under:
(a) Regulatory function
(b) Development function
(c) Protective function
(d) None of the above

32. Controlling Insider Trading and imposing penalties for such practices comes under the preview of which function of SEBI:
(a) Development (b) Regulatory
(c) Protective (d) All of above

33. Delivery of shares sold or payment of cash for shares bought is made on
(a) Pay in day (b) Pay out day
(c) Both (a) & (b) (d) None of above.

34. Registration of brokers and sub-brokers and other players in the market is __________ Function of SEBI.
(a) Regulatory (b) Protective
(c) Development (d) All of above

35. The economic condition of every country is reflected by dealings in
(a) Primary market (b) Stock market
(c) Money market (d) None of above

36. Which market directly contributes for capital formation and increase in capital of a firm.
(a) Secondary market (b) Primary market
(c) Both (a) & (b) (d) None of above

37. Match the method of Floatation of a company in column I with suitable examples in column II:

	Column –I		Column -II
A.	Prospectus	(i)	First ask the existing share holders to apply for new issue as per the directions under companies Act
B.	E IPO	(ii)	Invitation to public to apply shares through public notice
C.	Private Placement	(iii)	On line system of stock exchange
D.	Right Issue	(iv)	Offer the entire new issue to LIC

Choose the correct answer:
(a) A (i), B (iii), C (ii), D (iv)
(b) A (ii), B (iii), C (iv), D (i)
(c) A (iii), B (ii), C (i), D (iv)
(d) A (i), B (ii), C (iv), D (iii)

CHAPTER 11

Marketing

KEY POINTS

- **Term Market**
  - Product, Geographic, Types of buyers, quantity of goods sold.
  - Marketing and its features

(i) Needs and Wants

(ii) Creating a Market Offering

(iii) Customer Value

(iv) Exchange Mechanism

  - What can be marketed and who is a Marketer.
  - Difference between Marketing and Selling.

(i) Part of the process vs wider term

(ii) Transfer of title vs satisfying customer needs

(iii) Profit through maximising sales vs customer satisfaction

(iv) Start and End of the activities

(v) Difference in the emphasis

(vi) Difference in the strategies

- **Marketing Management Philosophies**
  - Production Concept
  - Product Concept
  - Selling Concept
  - Marketing Concept
  - Societal Marketing Concept
- **Functions of Marketing**
  - Gathering and analysing market information
  - Marketing planning
  - Product Designing and Development
  - Standardisation and Grading
  - Packaging and Labelling
  - Branding
  - Customer Support Services
  - Pricing of Product
  - Promotion
  - Physical Distribution
  - Transportation
  - Storage or Warehousing
- **Role of Marketing**
  - Role in firm
  - Role in the Economy
- **Marketing Mix**
  - **Elements of Marketing Mix**

(i) Product

(ii) Place

(iii) Price

(iv) Promotion

- **Classification of Products**
  - **Consumers Products**

(i) Shopping Efforts Involved

(ii) Durability of Product

(iii) Services

- **Industrial products**

(i) Material and parts

(ii) Capital items

(iii) Business Services

➤ **Branding**

- Brand
- Brand Name
- Brand Mark
- Trade Mark

➤ **Advantages to Marketers, Customers**

➤ **Characteristics of Good Brand Name**

➤ **Packaging**

- **Packaging Levels**

(i) **Primary**

(ii) **Secondary**

- **Importance and Functions**

Importance

(i) Health & Sanitation Standard

(ii) Self Service Outlet

(iii) Innovational Opportunity

(iv) Product Differentiation

Functions

(i) Product Identification

(ii) Product Protection

(iii) Facilitating use of the product

(iv) Product Promotion

➤ **Labelling Functions**

- Describe and specify the content of product
- Brand
- Grading of product
- Promotion of product
- Providing information required by law

➤ **Pricing ⟶ Factors affecting fixation of the price of product**

- Product cost
- Utility and Demand
- Extent of Competition in the Market
- Government and legal regulation
- Pricing objectives
- Marketing methods used

➤ **Pricing objectives**

- Market share leadership
- Surviving in a competitive market
- Attaining product quality

➤ **Physical Distribution**

Channels of Distribution – Types of Channel Direct Channel (zero) and Indirect Channel

Example of Indirect Channel are: one level, two level, three level channel

➤ **Promotion Mix – Meaning & Types**

- **Advertising**
- **Personal Selling**
- **Public Relations**
- **Sales Promotion**

➤ **Meaning, merits & limitation of each tool of promotion mix.**

➤ **Sales promotion activities meaning and examples**

- Rebate
- Discount
- Refunds
- Product Combinations
- Quantity Gift

- Instant Draws and Assigned Gift
- Lucky Draw
- Usable Benefit
- Full Finance @ 0%
- Sampling
- Contests

➤ **Publicity – Feature**

➤ **Public Relations – Role & Functions**

- Press relations
- Product publicity
- Corporate communication
- Lobbying
- Counselling

➤ **Advertising – Distinguishing feature**

➤ **Difference between Personal Selling and Advertising**

MCQs

1. Product, price, place and promotion are part of
   (a) Product Mix (b) Marketing Mix
   (c) Price Mix (d) Place Mix
2. What can be marketed? Choose the correct answer:
   (a) Product
   (b) Services
   (c) Idea
   (d) Anything which has value to others
3. Marketing is:
   (a) Pre-production activity
   (b) Post production activity
   (c) After sales activity
   (d) All of the above
4. Convincing, luring, attracting customers to buy a product, which marketing philosophy Is, highlighted here:
   (a) Selling concept (b) Product concept
   (c) Marketing concept (d) Production concept
5. When target customers are cost conscious and availability in quantity needs to be emphasised, which marketing philosophy is used:
   (a) Product (b) Production
   (c) Selling (d) Marketing
6. Product improvement is the key to profit maximisation of a firm. This statement throws light on which marketing philosophy?
   (a) Product (b) Selling
   (c) Marketing (d) Production
7. Assertion (A): The basic role of a firm is to 'Identify a need and fill it'.
   Reason (R): A pre requisite for the success of the firm and to earn profit ,an organisation has to understand and respond to the customers need and also that of the society's interest at large.
   (a) Both (A) and (R) are true and (R) is the correct explanation of A.
   (b) Both (A) and (R) are true and (R) is not the correct explanation of A.
   (c) A is true but R is false.
   (d) A is false but R is true.

Read the text and answer the Questions 8 & 9 below:

'Very tasty' MASALA was introduced by Masala & Herbs Co. Ltd. 'Very Tasty, after its launch, did not take much time to get very popular. The reason was because of one of its ingredient that it gave food very bright colour and taste to the food. The company enjoyed its record sales. However, they missed giving a statutory warning on the cover of the packet that *'Use of this masala in the long run is injurious to health'*.

8. Which concept is overlooked in this case:
   (a) Marketing concept
   (b) Societal marketing concept
   (c) Product concept
   (d) Selling concept
9. Identify the important element of product concept neglected by the marketer in the above case:
   (a) Packaging (b) Labelling
   (c) Branding (d) Grading
10. Packaging is called silent salesman because:
    (a) Attractive, colourful packing attracts the customers and induces them to buy.
    (b) Handling of the products becomes convenient.
    (c) Product differentiation becomes easy.
    (d) Products remain fresh.
11. Which element of product concept helps in fulfilling the right to information:
    (a) Branding (b) Labelling
    (c) Packaging (d) All of above
12. A farmer grows Organic carrots for the purpose of exports. He has fixed standards Eg. Good, Average, Reject. Accordingly, he has fixed

price for each particular quality of his product. This example throws light on which function of marketing management

(a) Grading & standardisation

(b) Product development and design

(c) Marketing planning

(d) None of above

13. Match the Branding related terms in column-I to its close meaning in column-II.

	Column-I		Column-II
I.	Brand	(1)	that part of brand which is not spoken but identified with sign or symbols
II.	Brand Name	(2)	Any term, name, sign, symbol, design or combination of them to identify the product.
III.	Brand Mark	(3)	A brand or part of brand which gives legal, exclusive right to its use
IV.	Trade Mark	(4)	This is verbal component of a brand.

Choose the answer:

(a) I (1) II (3) III (4) IV (2)

(b) I (4) II (2) III (1) IV (3)

(c) I (2) II (4) III (1) IV (3)

(d) I (3) II (1) III (2) IV (4)

14. Gathering and Analysing information is called:

(a) Marketing Research (b) Standardisation

(c) Promotion (d) None of these

15. A good brand should be:

(a) Short and easy to pronounce

(b) Suggesting product benefits

(c) Distinctive

(d) All of these

16. Packaging is important due to:

(a) Minimum chances of adulteration

(b) Product differentiation

(c) Promoting product

(d) All of above

17. The pricing strategy wherein *a low initial price is fixed to capture a large market share* is called:

(a) Penetration price

(b) Skim the cream pricing

(c) Both of the above (a) & (b)

(d) None of above

18. When demand of a product is inelastic, the firm should fix

(a) Higher price (b) Market price

(c) Lower price (d) None of these

19. Which of these is not a technique of Sales Promotion:

(a) Quantity gifts (b) Free samples

(c) Lucky Draw (d) Advertising

20. Price Mix refers to decision related to fixing of price of a commodity. This relates to

(a) Demand of product

(b) Price level of competition

(c) Cost

(d) All of above

Read the text and answer the questions 21 to 26 below:

Rahul and Mohan are brothers who work with their father in his Tea business in Assam.

They have a shop in the center of the city 'Nath & Sons', where different varieties of tea are sold.

Rahul and Mohan want to expand and start something new in their tea business. For this they do some market research, collect data from new and old target customers.

Researches revealed that having a Tea parlour was the latest fad among young population. They grabbed the idea and 'Superr Chhai Parlour' was established in place of 'Nath & Sons'.

This air conditioned parlour had sitting area and offered whole range of teas. Also tea packets were sold in the gallery of the palour. The tea packets were sold by the name 'Superr Chhai' - from small 100 gms packs to big 1 kg pkts. These packets were attractive, vaccum sealed, totally environment friendly soft packs.

Using their fathers knowledge & experience, they purchased good quality teas from auction and stored it in their warehouses and did their own blending and packaging. They also set an on line trading portal and would address any grievances and complaints.

21. Identify the marketing function used for conducting survey to collect data:
   (a) Transport
   (b) Warehousing
   (c) Gathering & analysing information
   (d) None of above.

22. Identify marketing function which they are performing by setting an online complaint portal:
   (a) Labelling
   (b) Transport
   (c) Customer support services
   (d) Branding

23. Use of online portal for trading and grievances indicate which dimension of business environment:
   (a) Social (b) Technological
   (c) Economic (d) Political

24. Name of the marketing philosophy used by Rahul & Mahesh
   (a) Production (b) Marketing
   (c) Societal Marketing (d) All of above

25. Highlight the function showing the name of their product.
   (a) Branding (b) Designing
   (c) Labelling (d) All of above

26. Identify the function of marketing which talks about storage of their product.
   (a) Transport (b) Labelling
   (c) Branding (d) Warehousing

27. ___________Philosophy of marketing focuses on intensive promotional tools.
   (a) Marketing concept (b) Product concept
   (c) Selling concept (d) Production concept

28. Which of the following is not a function of labelling.
   (a) Product protection
   (b) Product Description & content
   (c) Product grading
   (d) Information required by law.

29. The communication tool which helps in improving the image of the company is
   (a) Advertisement (b) Sales promotion
   (c) Personal selling (d) Public Relations

30. `You do not close a sale you open relationship if you want to build a long term successful enterprise'. Identify the promotion tool referred in this:
   (a) Advertisement (b) Sales promotion
   (c) Personal selling (d) Public Relation

31. Assertion (A): Advertisement is the paid form of non-personal presentation and promotion of idea, goods & services by an identified sponsor.
   Reason (R): The advertisement builds pull effect as advertising tries to pull the product by directly appealing to customers to buy it.
   (a) Both Assertion (A) & Reason (R) are correct and R is the correct explanation of A.
   (b) Both (A) & (R) are correct but R is not the correct explanation of A.
   (c) Both (A) & (R) are incorrect
   (d) (A) is correct but (R) is incorrect.

Read the Text and answer the questions 32-38 below:

Nidhi is a young MBA graduate, Married and joined her husband in Bangalore. She started working as a Manager in a leading food chain company. After the birth of her daughter, she had to quit her job. Looking at the busy schedule of all working women in her areas, she realised there was a need for a safe, healthy food outlet. She stumbled upon an idea,which she discussed with her friends & family and decided to Start her own Eatery – Samosa under the brand name of 'Bigg Samosa'. Samosas being a popular Indian snack it was warmly welcomed by people in her locality. She hired two cooks and sold Non-vegetarian and Vegetarian samosas on telephonic order to start with . All home delivered in self created environment friendly packets with their product name printed on the packets. This was a good way to advertise of her venture. 'Nothing beats like word of mouth in India. 'Her product became very popular in short time and her demand rose many times. She developed whatsapp network connecting prospective customers highlighting her newly added products with their prices.

With passage of time her business grew many fold and her products were also available 'On line' for sale. Orders from school canteen and offices, Kitty & birthday parties were indicating of her success story.

32. Highlight the function of marketing discussed above.
    (a) Packaging (b) Market Research
    (c) Branding (d) All of above

33. Identify the marketing concept used here:
    (a) Production (b) Product
    (c) Sales (d) Marketing

34. Which elements of promotion mix was used here:
    (a) Personal selling
    (b) Advertising
    (c) Both (a) & (b) above
    (d) None of above

35. The channel of distribution applied by Nidhi was
    (a) One level (b) Two level
    (c) Zero level (d) None of above

36. Use of WhatsApp and On-line portal for trading indicate which dimension of business Environment.
    (a) Social (b) Technological
    (c) Economic (d) Political

37. The brand 'Bigg Samosa" satisfies which of the following characteristic of a good brand name:
    (a) It should be short and easy to pronounce
    (b) It should be capable of being registered
    (c) A brand name should be distinct
    (d) All of above.

38. Which tool of promotion Mix was not seen in the above example
    (a) Advertising (b) Personal selling
    (c) Sales promotion (d) None of above

39. A firm desires to get quick rise in sales with immediate effect for a short period, then firm should use which method:
    (a) Advertisement (b) Personal selling
    (c) Sales promotion (d) Public Relation

40. Physical distribution is concerned with goods available at:
    (a) Right place (b) Right time
    (c) Both (a) & (b) (d) None of these

CHAPTER 12

Consumer Protection

KEY POINTS

- **Meaning and Importance of Consumers Protection**

Importance

- **From Consumer point of view**

(i) Consumer Ignorance

(ii) Unorganised Consumers

(iii) Widespread Exploitation of Consumers

- **From Business point of view**

(i) Long term Interest of business

(ii) Business uses Society's resources

(iii) Social Responsibility

(iv) Moral Justification

(v) Government Intervention

- **Legal protection to consumers [10 Acts]**
  - The Consumer Protection Act 1986
  - The Indian Contract Act 1872
  - The Sale of Goods Act 1930
  - The Essential Commodities Act 1955
  - The Agricultural Produce Act 1937
  - The Prevention of Food Adulteration Act 1954
  - The Standards of Weights and Measures Act 1976
  - The Trade Marks Act 1999
  - The Competition Act 2002
  - The Bureau of Indian Standards Act 1986

- **The Consumer Protection Act, 1986**

Consumer Rights

- Right to Safety
- Right to be Informed
- Right to Choose
- Right to be Heard
- Right to Seek Redressal
- Right to Consumer Education

- **Consumer Responsibilities**
  - Awareness of various goods available in market
  - Buy only standardised goods
  - Knowledge of risk associated with products
  - Read labels carefully of products
  - Asset yourself to get a fair deal
  - Choose only from legal goods and services
  - Ask for cash memo on purchase
  - File a complaint in an appropriate consumer forum
  - Form consumer societies for educating consumers
  - Respect the environment

- **Ways and Means of Consumer**
  - Self regulation by business
  - Business Associations
  - Consumer Awareness
  - Consumer Organisations
  - Government

➤ **Redressal Agencies**

Redressal Agencies under Consumer Protection Act

District Forum

↓

State Commission

↓

National Commission

↓

Supreme Court

➤ **Who is a consumer**

- **Who can file a complaint**

(i) Any consumer can file a complaint on his own

(ii) Any registered Consumer association

(iii) Central government or State government

(iv) One or more consumers on behalf of others

(v) A legal heir or representative of deceased consumer

(vi) A complaint under sec 2(b) of the Consumer Protection Act 1986

➤ **Relief Available**

- To remove the defect in goods or service
- To replace with new one
- To refund the price paid for product
- To pay reasonable amount of compensation for the loss
- To pay punitive damages in appropriate circumstances
- To discontinue the unfair practice
- Not to offer such goods for sale
- Withdraw such items from sale
- To cease manufacture of such goods
- To issue corrective advertisement

➤ **Role of Consumer Ogranisation and NGOs**

- Educate the general public about consumer rights
- Publishing periodicals to impart knowledge
- Carrying out comparative testing of consumer products and publishing the test results.
- Encouraging consumers to protest and take action
- Providing legal assistance to consumers
- Filing complaints in appropriate consumer courts
- Filing cases in consumer courts on the behalf of the public

➤ **Some Important Consumer NGOs are:**

- CCC (Delhi)
- VOICE (Delhi)
- CPC (Ahmedabad)
- CERC (Ahmedabad)
- CGSI (Mumbai)
- CUTS (Jaipur)
- Consumers Association (Kolkata)
- KCS (Bangalore)

MCQs

1. Right of Information Act came into force from:
   (a) 2004 (b) 1955
   (c) 1930 (d) 2002
2. This Act provides setting up of a three tier machinery for redressal of consumer grievences. The name of Act is ______
   (a) The Indian contract Act
   (b) The consumer protection Act
   (c) Essential Commodies Act
   (d) The Competition Act
3. Consumer rights cannot be effective in providing consumer protection unless ______ also understood their responsibilities
   (a) Seller (b) Consumer
   (c) Government (d) Consumer forum
4. Many consumer organisations encourage consumers to strongly protest against exploitative and unfair trade and file complaint. This is seen in
   (a) Right to be heard
   (b) Right to seek redressal
   (c) Right to safety
   (d) all of above
5. Informing consumers about their rights and relief available is part of
   (a) Right to safety
   (b) Right to Information
   (c) Right to consumer education
   (d) Right to be heard
6. Consumer protection Act is applicable to
   (a) Movable goods
   (b) Specific goods & services
   (c) Immovable goods
   (d) All goods & services
7. Which of the following is importance of consumer protection in view of business?
   (a) Moral Justification
   (b) Consumer ignorance
   (c) Unorganised consumers
   (d) Wide spread exploitation of consumers
8. To avail the benefit of consumer protection Act, the consumer
   (a) Must have a proof of purchase eg Cash Memo.
   (b) Choose legal goods and services
   (c) Buy standardised goods
   (d) All of above
9. Which of the following is importance of consumer protection in view of consumer
   (a) Consumer ignorance
   (b) Government intervention
   (c) Social Responsibility
   (d) Moral Justification
10. Who is not considered a consumer as per CPA 2019.
   (a) One who buys goods and/or hires services
   (b) Anyone who buys goods for earning livelihood.
   (c) The person who obtains goods for resale.
   (d) Person who buys goods for a consideration.
11. Match different *Marks of Quality* in Column-I with their associated products in column-II:

Column-I		Column-II	
1.	ISI	(i)	Environmental friendly product
2.	AGMARK	(ii)	Gold jewellary
3.	BIS Mark (Hall mark)	(iii)	Consumer durable products
4.	Ecomark	(iv)	On agricultural commodities and livestock products

   Choose the correct answer:
   (a) 1 (iii) 2 (iv) 3 (ii) 4 (i)
   (b) 1 (ii) 2 (iii) 3 (iv) 4 (i)
   (c) 1 (iv) 2 (iii) 3 (ii) 4 (i)
   (d) 1 (iii) 2 (ii) 3 (iv) 4 (i)
12. Name the Consumer court where the complain can be filed by the consumer:

(a) District forum (b) State Commission
(c) National Commission (d) All of above.

13. Department of consumer affairs has been undertaking the campaign through multimedia awareness namely
    (a) Aap ki Adalat (b) Jago Grahak Jago
    (c) Upbhokta Jagran (d) None of above

14. What are the major activities of Bureau of Indian Standard Act ?
    (a) Formation of quality standards for goods
    (b) Certification of goods through BIS
    (c) Both (a) & b) above
    (d) None of above

15. 'Jago Grahak Jago' - advertisement is highlighting which consumer right
    (a) Right to consumer Education
    (b) Right to Safety
    (c) Right to Information
    (d) Right to be heard

16. Labelling a component of product mix help the consumers to exercise
    (a) Right to Safety
    (b) Right to Information
    (c) Right to consumer Education
    (d) right to be heard

17. Match the Consumer Rights in Column-I with their explanation in Column-II:

	Column-I		Column-II
A.	Right to Information	1.	It informs consumer about their rights. This is given by NGO, Govt., etc.
B.	Right to Consumer Education	2.	It gives right to get compensation for damages suffered.
C.	Right to be heard	3.	It informs about the product, its content, use etc. This is given by manufacturer etc.
D.	Right to seek Redressal	4.	It is concerned with filing of complaint, manufacturer gives toll free number, set special counter for it.

Choose the correct answer:

(a) A - 2, B - 1, C - 3, D - 4
(b) A - 3, B - 1, C - 4, D - 2
(c) A - 4, B - 2, C - 1, D - 3
(d) A - 3, B - 2, C - 4, D - 1

18. Who can be a judge of state Commission.
    (a) Retired or working Judge of District commission
    (b) Retired or working Judge of National commission
    (c) Both (a) & (b)
    (d) None of above

19. District Court can entertain complaints where value of goods or services does not exceed ______.
    (a) 10 crore (b) 1 crore
    (c) 5 crore (d) None of above

20. Any person who is aggrieved by the order of State Commission can appeal against such order to National Commission within ______.
    (a) 30 days (b) 45 days
    (c) 90 days (d) 15 days

21. The role of consumer organisation and NGO in the field of consumer protection is not to ______.
    (a) Educate the villagers/ general public
    (b) Filing complaints in consumer courts on behalf of customers.
    (c) Prohibit people from protesting against exploitation and unfair trade practices
    (d) Publishing periodicals to impart knowledge about consumer problems.

22. Under Consumer protection Act, a consumer has been provided:
    (a) 4 rights (b) 6 rights
    (c) 8 rights (d) 3 rights

23. The earlier approach of Caveat Emptor which means, let the buyer beware has now been changed to
    (a) Let the seller beware

(b) Let the consumer beware

(c) Let the producer beware

(d) None of above

24. In developing countries like India the number of consumer organisations are very less. This is related to which importance of consumer protection.

(a) Wide spread exploitation of consumers

(b) Consumer ignorance

(c) Unorganised consumers

(d) None of above

25. The Consumer Protection Act, 2019 has replaced which Act?

(a) The CPA 1982 (b) The CPA 1984

(c) The CPA 1986 (d) The CPA 1988

CHAPTER 13

Entrepreneurship Development

1. Name the person who first introduced term **Entrepreneur**.
   (a) Peter Drucker (b) Adam Smith
   (c) Richard Cantillon (d) Joseph Schumpeter
2. Joseph A Schumpeter assigned a crucial role to entrepreneur,which is:
   (a) Motivation (b) Innovation
   (c) Inventer (d) Organiser
3. One best difference between ordinary risk and uncertainty is
   (a) Risk can be estimated while uncertainty cannot
   (b) Risk can be reduced through Insurance principles but uncertainty cannot be calculated so can't be insured.
   (c) Possible outcome in risks is known.
   (d) None of above
4. The essential elements of an entrepreneur are:
   (a) Innovation, Organiser, Motivation
   (b) Invention, Coordinator, Organiser
   (c) Risk Bearing, Organizing, Innovating
   (d) Coordinating, Organizing, Risk Bearing
5. Which of the following is not a personal characteristics of successful entrepreneur.
   (a) Desire & foresight for high achievement
   (b) Fearful thinking
   (c) Innovation
   (d) Independence
6. ________classified Entrepreneur, into four types.
   (a) Kilby (b) Clarence Danhof
   (c) Schumpeter (d) Jean Baptiste Say
7. An Entrepreneur who introduces new goods, new methods of production, new markets when certain level of development is already there, is called ___________.
   (a) Innovative (b) Initative
   (c) Fabian (d) Drone
8. One who is suitable for under-developed region, for bringing a mushroom drive of imitation of new combination of factors of production, are called ________ entrepreneur.
   (a) Innovator (b) Imitative
   (c) Fabian (d) Drone
9. ________ entrepreneur are those who are very cautious and skeptic in experimenting any change in the enterprise.
   (a) Innovator (b) Imitative
   (c) Fabian (d) Drone
10. ___________ entrepreneur are those who do not adopt opportunities to make change in production even at the cost of suffering losses.
   (a) Innovator (b) Imitation
   (c) Fabian (d) Drone
11. Fill in the blanks choosing from options:–Active, Solo, Partner
   (i) Entrepreneur who work alone. ________
   (ii) Entrepreneur who work alone or carry out as a joint venture. _________
   (iii) Those who only contribute funds but do not actively participate in Business. _________

   ***Choose the correct answer*:-**
   (a) (i) Solo (ii) Active (iii) Partner
   (b) (i) Active (ii) Solo, (iii) Partner
   (c) (i)Partner (ii) Solo (iii)Active
   (d) (i) Active (ii) partner (iii) Solo
12. Disneyland is example of which entrepreneurship.
   (a) Imitation (b) Drone
   (c) Innovation (d) Fabian

13. Indian Entrepreneurial Development Institute is situated in
(a) Ahmedabad (b) Mumbai
(c) New Delhi (d) Chennai

14. Risk bearers in a Company are
(a) Manager (b) Intrapreneur
(c) Entrepreneur (d) Suppliers

15. Country's progress can only be possible with the development of Entrepreneurship because they provide ____________
(a) Innovation
(b) Employment opportunities
(c) Inclusive growth
(d) All of above

16. Entrepreneur are related to internal factors,what are they:-
(a) Personality of an individual
(b) Psychological in nature
(c) Self Motivation
(d) All of above

17. Statement A: The future is heavily weighed in favour of knowledge Based Business (KBB)
Statement B: The life cycle of technology is getting shorter. New enterprise must have Knowledge of latest technology.
(a) Both statements A and B are correct
(b) Both statement A & B are wrong
(c) A is correct and B is wrong
(d) B is correct and A is wrong

18. Munnabai Dabbahwalah are example of what kind of entrepreneur.
(a) Product Based Business
(b) Idea Centric
(c) Trading
(d) Agricultural Business

19. Which one is not entrepreneurial competencies:
(a) Initiative
(b) Creativity & Innovation
(c) Problem solving & Risk
(d) Pervasive attitude

20. Point out who is not the First generation entrepreneur
(a) Dhirubhai Ambani
(b) Naresh Goyal
(c) N.R. Narayan Murthy
(d) Mahima Mehra

21. Corporate Entrepreneurship means:
(a) Innovations of some corporate of companies, leading to new venture.
(b) Some managers use systems in an unusual way to get a new product.
(c) Some new ventures provide new services.
(d) All of above.

22. Mc Clelland's 'Acquired Need theory' speaks about:
(a) Needs are to some extent acquired and so one can influence these needs
(b) Can be used with employees for greater involvement .
(c) Needs which motivate people are Achievement, Affiliation & power
(d) All of above.

23. Which Entrepreneurial competencies is seen in case of Steve Jobs 'Apple and I Pod'.
(a) Persistence
(b) Quality performance
(c) Motivation
(d) Initiative

24. Laggards is a term used for:
(a) Fabian (b) Drone
(c) Innovative (d) Initiative

25. Who are women entrepreneurs? They are firms where
(a) Minimum 51% of the capital owned & controlled by women with minimum 51% women employment.
(b) Minimum 51% of capital owned by women and 100% women employment.
(c) Minimum 100% of capital owned by women and 51% women employment.
(d) None of above.

Answers

Chapter - 1. Nature & Principles of Management

1. (d) Important for management to be equally effective and efficient and also at times it has to compromise with efficiency.
2. (d) all of above
3. (d) All of the above
4. (a) They interact and pass on instructions to the actual work force.
5. (a) Functions of management
6. (a) Planning
7. (d) controlling
8. (b) The essence of management
9. (d) All of the above
10. (b) Specialisation
11. (a) Theoretical knowledge and personalised application
12. (c) Management is a dynamic function
13. (b) Co-ordination is not the primary function
14. (d) Open entry. Entry is not open to all
15. (b) In middle management one sees divisional heads.
16. (b) Staffing function.
17. (d) All of the above
18. (c) Co-ordination helps in realisation of unity of action.
19. (d) All of the above
20. (b) Organising
21. (b) Management is a group activity.
22. (b) Rajiv is effective but not efficient
23. (a) Top level is responsible for the survival of the organisation.
24. (b) All pervasive
25. (b) Management of people
26. (a) Social objective
27. (d) Management
28. (c) Both (a) & b) above -> systematic working orderliness and co-ordination in working environment.
29. (b) Management as an art.
30. (d) Management helps in achieving personal goals.
31. (d) All of the above
32. (a) Social objective
33. (b) Series of functions
34. (d) Number of creditors
35. (d) All of above functions
36. (a) Both (A) & (R) are true

Chapter - 2. Principles of Management

1. (d) Contingent
2. (a) Chain of authority and communication.
3. (b) Flexible
4. (b) Mining Engineer
5. (d) They are developed by observation and experience of mangers.
6. (b) Equity
7. (b) Rest pauses are decided by fatigue study.
8. (d) Centralisation and Decentralisation.
9. (c) It is extension of principle of division of work.
10. (d) All of the above

11. (b) Science not rule of thumb is the scientific management principle.
12. (b) Rs. 1315
13. (d) All of the above
14. (b) Principle of Equity
15. (b) Plan, Organise, Command, Co-ordinate and Control.
16. (d) All points in a + b + c given above.
17. (c) 14 principles
18. (c) Gang boss
19. (b) Simplification and Standardisation of Work.
20. (b) Co-operation not Individualism.
21. (c) Stability of tenure of Personnel.
22. (d) Espirit de corps
23. (a) Employees working at the same level.
24. (c) Inspector is a foreman responsible for quality of work.
25. (b) Differential piece rate system
26. (d) All of the above
27. (c) Both (a) and (b) points above.
28. (a) Remuneration of Employees principle
29. (b) De-motivation of employees.
30. (d) (i & iv) above. Work should be divided into small tasks and It leads to specialisation
31. (d) All of the above
32. (b) Authority and Responsibility
33. (a) Centralisation and Decentralisation
34. (b) Unity of Command
35. (a) Planning, Execution
36. (d) Both A & R are correct and R is not the correct explanation of A.
37. (c) Both A & R are correct and R is the correct explanations of A.

Chapter - 3. Business Environment

1. (c) Business Environment is not simple in fact it is dynamic and uncertain.
2. (d) All of above i.e. improve quality of product, reduction in cost and to engage aggressive advertising.
3. (a) Dynamic and inter-relatedness.
4. (i) (a) Social Environment
   (ii) (a) Economic Environment
5. (c) Discriminatory employment is not an example of values.
6. (d) All of the above – Get first mover advantage identify early warning signals, adjust to rapid changes.
7. (d) Economic Environment
8. (b) Political Environment
9. (c) Economic Environment
10. (d) Legal Environment
11. (a) Assisting in planning and policy making.
12. (d) All of above in Govt. Policies, Technological Development and Political Stability.
13. (c) Social environment
14. (c) Requirement of permission for technology agreement with foreign countries.
15. (a) Liberalisation
16. (a) Specific and General forces.
17. (a) Helps in coping with rapid change.
18. (c) Both (a) and (b) above. Improving tax compliances and savings through the formal financial system.
19. (b) Reduced government controls and restrictions.
20. (b) Public sector wealth.
21. (a) 8th Nov., 2016

22. (a) Firms have to study and analyse the market first to produce goods accordingly.

23. (c) change in agricultural prices.

24. (c) Both (a) and (b) above i.e. loss of government budgetary support for financing and disinvestment.

25. (d) All of the above (a), (b) and (c).

26. (b) (i), (ii) and (iii) above i.e. Disinvestment of public sector, setting up of BIFR and Dilution of stake of Government.

27. (a) Specific

28. (b) A – (iii) B – (iv) C – (i) D – (ii)

Chapter - 4. Planning

1. (d) (a) and (b) both setting of objectives and formulation of an action plan.
2. (d) Planning
3. (d) All of the above
4. (c) Planning reduces risks of uncertainties.
5. (b) Mental Exercise
6. (d) All of the above. Competition in market, political condition and natural calamity.
7. (c) Planning
8. (a) Planning precedes other function.
9. (a) Creativity of workers.
10. (b) Policy – Retirement age of employees is 60 yrs.
11. (a) Both statement I and II is correct. This is because of the dynamic nature of business environment.
12. (d) Planning is closely connected with creativity and innovation.
13. (c) Identifying alternative course of action.
14. (c) Planning leads to rigidity.
15. (b) Viability of the plans may change due to unforeseen factors.
16. (b) Standing plan.
17. (b) A is correct and R is incorrect.
18. (b) I - D II - B III - A IV - C
19. (c) Follow up
20. (d) Selecting of alternatives
21. (c) Methods
22. (d) A and R are correct and (R) is the correct explanation of A.
23. (d) All of the above.
24. (c) Rule – pet animals are not allowed in some eatery joints & cafe.
25. (a) Creativity of Workers
26. (b) Planning reduces overlapping of activities.
27. (c) It may not work in dynamic environment.
28. (c) Programme
29. (a) Single use plan are used only once.
30. (b) Planning premises.

Chapter - 5. Organising

1. (d) All of the above
2. (c) Organising
3. (a) Functional provides benefits of occupational specialisation.
4. (c) Standardisation
5. (b) Number of subordinate that can be effectively managed by a superior.
6. (a) Divisional Structure
7. (d) Fair predictability of behaviour of employees.
8. (a) Authority is restricted by law.
9. (a) Both (A) and (R) are true and (R) is the correct explanation of (A).

10. (c) Prescribed lines of communication is not followed.
11. (c) Relief to top management.
12. (a) Both statement I and II are correct.
13. (d) All of the above
14. (d) A sound organisation structure will give specialisation, classification of authority and responsibility and avoiding of duplication of work.
15. (c) I - B II - C III - A IV - D
16. (d) Formal organisation is dependent on informal organisation.
17. (c) Better co-ordination amongst different departments.
18. (c) Not true statement — Authority should be more than responsibility.
19. (a) Both (A) and (R) are true and (R) is the correct explanation of A.
20. (a) Pitfall of organising is that — repetitive performance of the same job leads to Monotony and boredom.
21. (b) Wide span of management.
22. (c) Functional
23. (d) All of the above
24. (b) (iii), (ii), (i), (iv)
25. (b) A - (iv), B - (i), C - (ii), D - (iii)

Chapter - 6. Staffing

1. (b) Right person for the right job leads to higher performance.
2. (a) Staffing — Human Resources are our assets.
3. (c) Human Resources — Non financial parameter.
4. (d) All of the above
5. (b) It is essential function of manager and also has to play an advisory role.
6. (a) Workload analysis — Assessing the number and types of human resources necessary for performance of jobs.
7. (b) Work force analysis — Analysing existing employees.
8. (c) Standardisation
9. (c) Recruitment
10. (b) A (ii), B (i), C (iv), D (iii)
11. (d) It is very economical — is not a defect of internal sources of recruitment.
12. (c) Campus recruitment.
13. (a) Jobbers
14. (b) Selection
15. (d) Selection — It is called a negative process because it has to select a few and reject many.
16. (a) A-(iv), B-(i), C-(ii), D(iii)
17. (c) Orientation—This is a step of familiarisation of employees in a new organisation.
18. (b) Vacation + club membership + medical benefits.
19. (c) Combination of time and performance.
20. (b) Employment interviews.
21. (b) Contract of Employment.
22. (a) Education, Training.
23. (a) (iv), (i), (iii), (ii)
24. (c) Vestibule training.
25. (a) Job Rotation
26. (a) Apprenticeship program
27. (d) Development
28. (d) All of the above
29. (b) A-(iii), B-(iv), C-(i), D-(ii)
30. (d) All of the above
31. (a) On the Job training
32. (d) All of the above
33. (b) A-(iv), B-(iii), C-(i), D-(ii)

Chapter - 7. Direction

1. (c) Laissez — faire – free rein leader. No use of power unless it is absolutely essential.
2. (d) Stock option — is a financial incentives given to employees.
3. (b) Directing — Initiates action in an ogranisation.
4. (d) Directing includes all – Supervision, Leadership and Motivation.
5. (a) Motivation — is a element of Directing.
6. (c) External inputs do not assist in directing.
7. (d) Directing is performed at all levels.
8. (b) Motivation, Motive, Motivator
9. (b) Psychologist
10. (d) C - Basic Salary, E - Pension plan, D - Affiliation, A - Job title, B - Achievement of goal. So CEDAB as per Maslow theory.
11. (d) Leadership — Misbehaviour of the leader.
12. (d) All of the above steps
13. (b) Authoritarian
14. (b) Exchange views which can not be done in formal communication.
15. (c) Job Enrichment
16. (d) All of the above are non-financial incentive.
17. (d) Communication Skill
18. (b) Encoding is converting messages into communication.
19. (c) Wheel
20. (d) Organisational barrier.
21. (b) Sematic
22. (b) 1 - (iii), 2 - (iv), 3 - (i), 4 - (ii)
23. (c) Employee Recognition programme
24. (b) Pension and gratuity.
25. (b) Communication
26. (b) Informal communication is used to get the real feedback of employees by the manager.
27. (a) A - 4, B - 3, C - 1, D - 2
28. (a) The receiver of communication may also be encouraged to respond to the message.
29. (b) Democratic
30. (d) Directing takes place at all levels.

Chapter - 8. Controlling

1. (d) Controlling
2. (a) Planning and controlling are interdependent and inter related activities.
3. (c) Controlling is both backward looking and forward looking function.
4. (c) Controlling function
5. (c) It helps in accomplishing the organisation goals.
6. (b) Establishing reporting relationship.
7. (c) Both Qualitative and Quantitative.
8. (b) Management by exception.
9. (b) Below the permissible limit deviations should be ignored.
10. (a) Both (A) and (R) are true and (R) is the correct explanation of A.
11. (b) Taking corrective action.
12. (a) Actual performance.
13. (a) Critical areas.
14. (a) Controlling
15. (b) Judging accuracy of standard.

Chapter - 9. Financial Management

1. (d) All of the above
2. (a) Wealth maximization
3. (c) Investment decision
4. (d) Stock market operations
5. (a) Financing decision
6. (a) A - 2, B - 3, C - 1, D -4
7. (a) higher dividend when tax rates are low.
8. (c) Free legal policy is not a factor affecting dividend decision.
9. (b) Loan agreement may show restrictions on divided payment by financier.
10. (d) All of the above
11. (c) Both (a) and (b) above when earning potential has gone up and earning of current year alone is not the criteria for increased dividend.
12. (d) Capital Budgeting
13. (b) Firms retain earnings more and declare less dividend.
14. (b) Future prospects by forecasting of sales.
15. (c) High Debt Equity ratio results in higher degree of financial risks.
16. (a) Because payment of interest and repayment of principal is obligatory hence whether the firm makes profit or not they have to pay it. This makes debt risky.
17. (b) Level of Competition
18. (a) Debt
19. (b) High dividend so that retired people have some source of fund.
20. (a) Return on Investment
21. (a) Stock market condition is a factor relating to financing decision.
22. (b) Floatation Cost
23. (a) Longer the operating cycle, more the working capital requirement.
24. (a) No Floatation cost required in raising funds by debt.
25. (a) ROI should be higher than the rate of interest.
26. (c) Equity Trading
27. (c) Partly from both current liability and long term liability.
28. (a) WC = CA – CL
29. (d) All are long term sources of funds.
30. (b) $25\% = \frac{25}{100} \times 100$

    $ROI = \frac{EBITD}{Total\ Cap} \times 100.$
31. (d) All of the above.

Chapter - 10. Financial Market

1. (a) Money market
2. (d) All of above, linking saver & investor, enabling them to invest their surplus fund and also borrow funds.
3. (c) Bridge financing
4. (b) Money market
5. (a) 15 days to one year
6. (b) Rs. 25,000 minimum amount
7. (b) A - (ii), B - (iii), C - (iv), D - (i)
8. (d) Certificate of deposit
9. (a) 100 stock or less
10. (d) All of the above
11. (b) Commercial paper
12. (a) One year
13. (c) Commercial papers are not traded in capital market

14. (b) DFHI is Discount Finance Head of India
15. (b) Treasury Bills are issued by RBI
16. (b) Secondary Market for market of existing securities
17. (b) Right Issue
18. (d) All of the above
19. (b) SEBI
20. (c) Contract Note
21. (a) E A B F C D
22. (a) Serve as link between Investors and Depository.
23. (a) Electronic trading system is screen based trading.
24. (a) Clearing Corporations
25. (a) Both (A) and (R) are correct and R is the correct explanation of A.
26. (a) T + 1 (Recently changed from T + 2 on 25 Feb, 22.)
27. (b) 1994
28. (b) January, 1992
29. (b) NSDL
30. (b) De-materialisation
31. (b) Development function
32. (c) Protective
33. (a) Pay in day
34. (a) Regulatory
35. (b) Stock Exchange
36. (b) Primary Market
37. (b) A - (ii), B - (iii), C - (iv), D - (i)

Chapter - 11. Marketing

1. (b) Marketing Mix
2. (d) Anything which has value to others
3. (d) All of the above
4. (b) Product concept
5. (b) Production
6. (a) Product
7. (b) Both (A) and (R) are true but R is not the correct explanation of A.
8. (b) Societal Marketing Concept
9. (b) Labelling
10. (a) Attractive colourful packaging attracts the customers and induces them to buy.
11. (b) Labelling
12. (a) Grading and Standardisation
13. (c) I - 2, II - 4, III - 1, IV - 3
14. (a) Marketing Research
15. (d) All of these
16. (d) All of the above
17. (a) Penetration price
18. (a) Higher price
19. (d) Advertising
20. (d) All of the above
21. (a) Transport
22. (c) Customer Support Services
23. (b) Technological
24. (b) Marketing
25. (a) Branding
26. (d) Warehousing
27. (c) Selling concept
28. (a) Product protection
29. (d) Public Relations
30. (c) Personal Selling
31. (a) (A) and (R) are correct and R is the correct explanation of A.
32. (d) All of the above
33. (d) Marketing
34. (c) Both (a) & (b) above
35. (c) Zero Level
36. (b) Technological

37. (d) All of the above

38. (c) Sales Promotion

39. (c) Sales Promotion

40. (c) Both (a) and (b) i.e. Right place and Right time.

Chapter - 12. Consumer Protection

1. (a) 2004
2. (b) The Consumer Protection Act
3. (b) Consumer
4. (a) Right to be Heard
5. (c) Right to Consumer Education
6. (d) All goods and Services
7. (a) Moral Justification
8. (d) All of the above
9. (a) Consumer ignorance
10. (c) The person who obtains goods for Resale.
11. (a) 1 - (iii), 2 - (iv), 3 - (ii), 4 - (i)
12. (d) All of the above
13. (b) Jago Grahak Jago
14. (c) Both (a) and (b) above
15. (a) Right to Consumer Education
16. (b) Right to Information
17. (b) A - 3, B - 1, C - 4, D - 2
18. (b) Retired or working judge of National Commission
19. (b) 1 crore
20. (a) 30 days
21. (c) Prohibit people from protesting against exploitation and unfair trade practices.
22. (b) 6 rights
23. (a) Let the seller beware
24. (a) Widespread exploitation of consumers.
25. (c) The CPA 1986.

Chapter - 13. Entrepreneurship Development

1. (c) Richard Cantillon
2. (b) Innovation
3. (b) Risk case be reduced by Insurance principle but uncertainty cannot be calculated so can't be insured.
4. (c) Risk bearing, Organising, Innovating
5. (b) Fearful thinking
6. (b) Clarence Danhof
7. (a) Innovative
8. (b) Imitative
9. (c) Fabian
10. (d) Drone
11. (a) (i) Solo, (ii) Active, (iii) Partner
12. (c) Innovation
13. (a) Ahmedabad
14. (c) Entrepreneur
15. (d) All of above ie. Innovation Employment Opportunities and Inclusive growth.
16. (d) All of the above ie. Personality, Self motivation, Psychological in nature
17. (a) Both statements A and B are correct
18. (b) Idea Centric
19. (d) Pervasive attitude
20. (d) Mahima Mehra
21. (d) All of the (a), (b) and (c)
22. (d) All of the above
23. (b) Quality performance
24. (b) Drone
25. (a) Mini. 51% of capital owned and controlled by women with Mini. 51% of women employment.

SAMPLE QUESTION PAPER 1

Max Marks: 200 Time: 45 min.

General Instruction:

(i) This paper consists of 50 MCQs, attempt 40 out of 50

(ii) Correct answer or most appropriate answer: Five marks (+5)

(iii) Any incorrect option marked will be given minus one marks (–1)

(iv) Unanswer /Marked for review will be given no mark (0)

(v) If more than one option is found to be correct then Five marks (+5) will be awarded to only those who have marked any of the correct option.

(vi) If all options are found to be correct five marks (+5) will be awarded to all those who have attempted the question.

(vii) If none of the options is found correct or a Question is found to be wrong then all candidates who have appeared will be given five marks (+5).

(viii) Calculator/ any electronic gadgets are not permitted.

1. Management is multidimensional and it stands for
   (a) Management at work
   (b) Management of people
   (c) Management of operation
   (d) All of above

2. 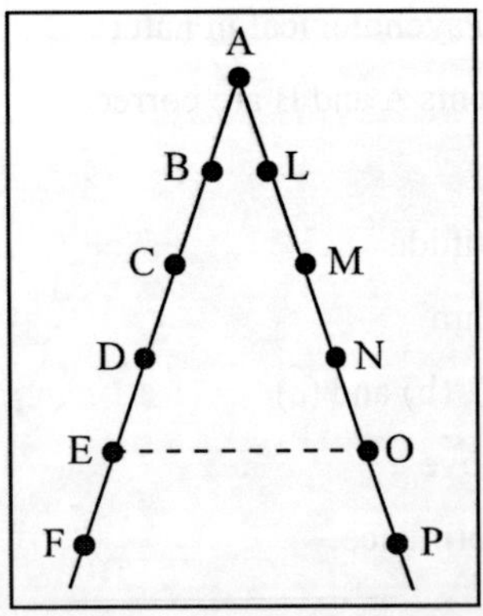

   The diagram refers to Fayol's principle of scalar chain which talks about
   (a) Chain of authority and communication.
   (b) Need to balance subordinate involvement through decentralisation.
   (c) All units of an organisation should be moving towards the same objective.
   (d) chain of authority and responsibility.

3. The organic food market in India is growing at a rate of 25% - 30%. This reflects a clear shift in consumers taste and preference. Identify the feature of business environment being referred here:
   (i) Dynamic nature
   (ii) Inter-relatedness
   (iii) Relatively.

   Choose the answer:
   (a) Points (i) & (ii) above
   (b) Points (ii) & (iii) above
   (c) Points (i) & (iii) above
   (d) All of above

4. Planning requires logical and systematic thinking. The feature of planning referred here is:

(a) Routine Activity

(c) Continuous process

(b) Mental Exercise

(d) All pervasive

5. The long term success of a company is usually examined on certain financial and non financial parameter. One such non-financial parameter is:

(a) Assets

(b) Capital Resources

(c) Human Resources

(d) Creditors

6. 'A good leader can identify the potential of his employees and encourages them to extract work up to their full potential'.

The element of directing highlighted here is

(a) Motivation (b) Leadership

(c) Supervision (d) Communication

7. The management function which ensures that efforts are directed towards the attainment of goals as per the plans:

(a) Directing (b) Controlling

(c) Staffing (d) Organising

8. The primary aim of financial management is best known by ___________ concept:

(a) Wealth maximization

(b) Cost minimization

(c) Investment maximization

(d) Profit maximization

9. Controlling is ___________

(a) Backward looking function

(b) Forward looking function

(c) Both forward and backward looking function

(d) None of the above

10. Product improvement is the key to profit maximisation of a firm. This throws light on which marketing philosophy:

(a) Product (b) Selling

(c) Marketing (d) Production

11. In financial market, instruments with maturity of less than one year is traded in

(a) Money market

(b) Capital market

(c) Primary market

(d) Industrial market

12. Many consumer organisations encourage consumers to strongly protest against exploitative and unfair trade and file complaint. This is seen in

(a) Right to be Heard

(b) Right to seek Redressal

(c) Right to Safety

(d) All of above

13. The most important function expected from a modern entrepreneur is _________

(a) Skill (b) Innovation

(c) Social skills (d) Fore sightedness

14. Which of this is not a characteristic of a profession?

(a) Professional association

(b) Ethical code of conduct

(c) Service motive

(d) Open entry

15. Taylor believed that efficiency can be maximized through Study and Analysis. **Identify the principle of Scientific management mentioned above:**

(a) Harmony not discord

(b) Science not Rule of thumb

(c) Co-operation not individualism

(d) Development of every person to the greatest efficiency.

16. Relaxation or removal of strict rules and regulations is part of

(a) Liberalization (b) Globalization

(c) Privatization (d) All of above

17. Match the term in Column I with suitable narration in Column II:

	Column-I		Column-II
I.	Policy	A.	Advertisement of BYJU classes during TATA IPL cricket matches
II.	Procedure	B.	Keeping the passport size photographs along with duly filled admission form in the admission file of the candidate.
III.	Strategy	C.	All mobiles to be switched off during meetings.
IV.	Rule	D.	Student securing 70% & above in Class X are eligible for admission in XI Science.

Choose the correct answer:

(a) I-A, II-C, III-B, IV-D

(b) I-D, II-B, III-A, IV-C

(c) I-B, II-A, III-D, IV-C

(d) I-C, II-D, III-A, IV-B

18. Decentralisation is greatest when checking required on decisions taken by lower levels is least.

This statement highlights one of the following:

(a) Quick decision making

(b) Better control

(c) Relief to top management

(d) Facilities growth

19. A document which contains vital details about the candidate and which is also authenticated and attested by him is called:

(a) Job offer

(b) Contract of employment

(c) Medical fitness Certificate

(d) Application form

20. Arrange the following needs of an employee working in an organisation on the basis of Maslow's Need of Hierarchy Theory.

A. Job Title B. Achievement of goals

C. Basic salary D. Affiliation

E. Pension plan

Choose the correct answer

(a) B, C, E, A, D (b) A, D, C, E, B

(c) B, C, D, A, E (d) C, E, D, A, B

21. Control should focus on key results area which are ________ to the success of an organisation.

(a) Critical (b) Flexible

(c) Involved (d) Consistent

Read the text and answer the questions 22, 23, 24 below:

Mr. Ranbir is the owner of 'Ranbir sports club' having facilities for different sports including football. Till now the company had been operating on owners' funds. Keeping in view of his plan to set up one more club, exclusive for football, in a different part of the city, the company raised debt capital to take advantage of trading on equity. The proportion of debt in the total capital of the company is 30% .the debt has been raised @ 12% whereas the return on investment is 10%, However, even after employing debt, the EPS' of the company is falling.

22. The factor which favoured the issue of debt by the company:

(a) No flotation cost

(b) Risk consideration

(c) Stock market condition

(d) Capital structure of other companies

23. The EPS of the firm is declining even after utilising debt, This is because ________

(a) ROI should be higher than the rate of interest.

(b) ROI should be same as rate of interest

(c) ROI and rate of interest are not affecting each other.

(d) None of the above.

24. The objective of Mr. Ranbir was to have a judicious mix of Owners' fund and Debt. The Proportion of Debt in overall capital is called ________

(a) Capital structure (b) Financial leverage

(c) Equity Trading (d) None of the above

25. Assertion: (A) Advertisement is the paid form of non-personal presentation and promotion of idea, goods & services by an identified sponsor.
Reason: (R) The advertisement builds pull effect, as advertising tries to pull the product by directly appealing to customers to buy it.
(a) Both Assertion (A) & Reason (R) are correct and R is the correct explanation of A.
(b) Both (A) & (R) are correct but R is not the correct explanation of A.
(c) Both (A) & (R) are incorrect
(d) (A) is correct but (R) is incorrect.

26. The apex body who controls the capital market of our country is:
(a) RBI (b) SBI
(c) SEBI (d) None of the above

27. What are the major activities of Bureau of Indian Standard Act ?
(a) Formulation of quality standard for goods
(b) Certification of goods through BIS
(c) Both a) & b) Above
(d) None of the above

28. Assertion: (A) The role of global manager has evolved in the same way as global industry and economy.
Reason: (R) Global manager has a multifaceted role, which requires diverse combination of skills.
(a) Both Assertion (A) and Reason (R) are correct and (R) is the correct explanation of (A)
(b) Both Assertion (A) and Reason (R) are correct and (R) is not the correct explanation of (A)
(c) Assertion (A) is incorrect but Reason (R) is correct.
(d) Assertion (A) is correct and Reason (R) are incorrect.

29. In Japanese Companies 'Paternalist style of management is in practice. This means that there is:
(a) Complete openness between management and workers.
(b) Employees take care of the needs of the employees
(c) Trade unions are not required
(d) All of the above

30. Zero defect zero effect model has a link with ________
(a) Privatization (b) Liberalisation
(c) Globalization (d) Digitalisation

31. Employees have to follow plans totally. This way planning reduces:
(a) Interest
(b) Application of knowledge
(c) Creativity of workers
(d) None of the above

32. Match the terms in Column I with suitable narration in Column II:

	Column-I		Column-II
I.	Delegation	A.	Arises from formal position.
II.	Decentralisation	B.	More control by superiors hence less freedom to take own decision.
III.	Authority	C.	It an optional policy decision. It is done at the discretion of the top management.
IV.	Responsibility	D.	Obligation to perform an assigned task.

Choose the correct answer:
(a) I-B, II-D, III-A, IV-C
(b) I-D, II-C, III-B, IV-A
(c) I-B, II-C, III-A, IV-D
(d) I-C, II-D, III-A, IV-B

33. Arrange the following steps in process of organising in the correct sequence.
(i) Assignment of duties
(ii) Departmentalization
(iii) Identification and division of work
(iv) Establishing reporting relationship

Choose the correct answer:

(a) (i), (ii), (iv), (iii)   (b) (iii), (ii), (i), (iv)

(c) (iii),(ii), (iv),(i)   (d) (ii),(iii),(i),(iv)

34. Match the meaning of concepts in Column I with concepts of Staffing in column II.

	Column-I		Column-II
I.	It is the process of identifying and choosing the most eligible one.	(i)	Recruitment
II.	Searching for the prospective candidates.	(ii)	Job Analysis
III.	Defining all content, authority and responsibility relating to the job	(iii)	Job specification
IV.	Qualification, attributes which a person must possess to apply for a job.	(iv)	Selection

Choose the right answer:

(a) I (iv), II (i), III (ii), IV (iii)

(b) I (iii), II (ii), III (i), IV (iv)

(c) I (i), II (iv), III (iii), IV (iv)

(d) I (iv), II (ii), III (iii), IV (i)

35. The focus of ______ is to develop logical and rational mind while the focus of ______ is to improve work efficiency.

Choose the correct answer:

(a) Education, Development

(b) Education, Training

(c) Training, Development

(d) Training, Education

36. Ranjan who works in a popular coffee house, gets selected for the 'Best Employee of the month'. His name and photograph is placed on the notice board of the cafe. He is also given a badge to wear stating 'Best Employee for that particular month'.

In the narration given above, giving such incentives are called:

(a) Job Enrichment

(b) Career Advancement opportunity

(c) Employee Recognition Programme

(d) Employee participation

37. A manager who tries to control everything ends up controlling nothing. This highlights the principle of

(a) Span of control

(b) Delegation of Authority

(c) Management by Exception

(d) Unity of command

38. A company's earnings before interest and tax is Rs 25 lakhs. It pays 10% interest on its debts. His total investment is Rs. 1 crore. Calculate the company's ROI.

(a) 20%   (b) 10%

(c) 25%   (d) 30%

39. ______________ is the technology driven electronic storage system promoted by NSE.

(a) CDSL   (b) SBI

(c) NSDL   (d) NYSE

40. Match the market instruments in Column I with the terms connected in Column II.

	Column-I		Column-II
A.	Commercial paper	(i)	Zero Coupon Bond
B.	Commercial Bill	(ii)	Bridge financing
C.	Call Money	(iii)	Trade Bill
D.	Treasury Bill	(iv)	Inter Bank Money Market

Choose the correct answer:

(a) A - (ii) B - (iii) C - (i) D - (iv)

(b) A - (ii) B - (iii) C - (iv) D - (i)

(c) A - (iv) B - (i) C - (iii) D - (ii)

(d) A - (i) B - (ii) C - (iii) D - (iv)

41. An entrepreneur who blindly follows traditional method of production in spite of loss is called ______________

(a) Innovative entrepreneur

(b) Drone Entrepreneur

(c) Fabian entrepreneur

(d) Adoptive entrepreneur

Read the text and answer Q 42, 43

"Very Tasty Masala" was introduced by Masala and Herbs Co. Ltd. 'Very Tasty' after its launch did not take much time to get very popular.

The reason was because of one of its ingredient which gave very bright colour and taste to the food. The company enjoyed its record success. However, they missed giving a statutory warning on the cover of this packet i.e. "Use of this masala in the long run can be injurious to health".

42. Which concept is overlooked in this case:-
    (a) Marketing concept
    (b) Societal Marketing concept
    (c) Product concept
    (d) Selling concept

43. Identify an important element of product concept neglected by a marketer in the above case:-
    (a) Packaging (b) Branding
    (c) Labelling (d) Grading

44. Which of the following are the functions of an entrepreneur:-
    (a) Risk assumption function
    (b) Decision Making function
    (c) Function of Innovation
    (d) All of above

45. Match the Column I showing Marks indicating Quality with different products in Column-II.

	Column-I		Column-II
I.	ISI	1.	Environment friendly product
II.	AGMARK	2.	Gold Jewellery
III.	BIS (Hallmark)	3.	Consumer durable products
IV.	ECOMARK	4.	On agricultural commodities and livestock products.

Choose the correct answer:-

(a) I (2), II (3), III (1), IV (4)
(b) I (4), II (3), III (1), IV (2)
(c) I (3), II (4), III (2), IV (1)
(d) I (2), II (3), III (1), IV (4)

46. Controlling Insider Trading and Imposing penalties for such practices comes under the preview of which function of SEBI:-
    (a) Development (b) Regulatory
    (c) Protective (d) All of above

47. The Communication gap due to size and complexity of organisation structure comes under which of the following categories:-
    (a) Psychological barrier
    (b) Personal barrier
    (c) Sematic barrier
    (d) Organisational barrier

48. A salesman of A B Engineering LTD could not achieve his sales target of 10,000 units. On enquiry it was found that he was not allowed to take decisions related to give discount and selling on credit to any of his earlier/new customers.

    The principle of management which is violated here:-
    (a) Discipline
    (b) Authority & Responsibility
    (c) Centralisation and Decentralisation
    (d) Principle of order

49. Who is not considered a 'Consumer' as per CPA 2019?
    (a) One who buys goods and/or hire services.
    (b) Anyone who buys goods for earning livelihood.
    (c) The person who obtains goods for resale.
    (d) Person who buys goods for consideration.

50. Screen based trading is called ______________
    (a) Private placement
    (b) Electronic trading system
    (c) Indirect trading
    (d) None of the above

SAMPLE QUESTION PAPER 2

Max Marks: 200 Time: 45 min.

General Instruction:

(i) This paper consists of 50 MCQs, attempt 40 out of 50

(ii) Correct answer or most appropriate answer = Five marks (+5)

(iii) Any incorrect option marked will be given minus one marks (–1)

(iv) Unanswer /Marked for review will be given no mark (0)

(v) If more than one option is found to be correct then Five marks (+5) will be awarded to only those who have marked any of the correct option.

(vi) If all options are found to be correct five marks (+5) will be awarded to all those who have attempted the question.

(vii) If none of the options is found correct or a Question is found to be wrong then all candidates who have appeared will be given five marks (+5).

(viii) Calculator/ any electronic gadgets are not permitted.

1. The activities of a Manager are inter-related. The above statement relates to
   (a) Functions of Management
   (b) Organisation of activities
   (c) Staffing of workforce
   (d) Operational Management

2. The complexities of modern technology and diversity of tasks to be performed leads to
   (a) Co-ordination (b) Specialisation
   (c) Management (d) None of above

3. The effect of Managerial principle varies from one situation to another. This is because it is related to one of the following characteristics of management principles.
   (a) Cause end effect relationship
   (b) Universal application
   (c) Flexible
   (d) Contingent

Read the text and answer the question 4 and 5: Manish Confectionaries was earlier supplying bakery products in New Delhi, Now with the Changing trend and consumption habits of the people of that locality they extended and modernized it into a café by the name Coffee and cake café (CCC) with a smart air conditioned sit in area. They along with bakery products also included certain popular snacks and coffee.

4. Identify the element of business environment discussed here:-
   (a) Social Environment
   (b) Political Environment
   (c) Legal Environment
   (d) Economic Environment

5. 'CCC' coffee and cake café also created their website and started taking on-line orders with free home delivery. Identify the dimension of Business Environment.
   (a) Legal (b) Economic
   (c) Technological (d) Political

6. Business Environment is dynamic. The heads in the Planning department do not get shocked with sudden changes. This highlights which of these points of importance of planning:
   (a) Planning facilities decision making
   (b) Planning promotes innovative ideas
   (c) Planning reduces risk of uncertainties
   (d) Planning provides direction

7. Which one is not the step of organising process:
   (a) Departmentalisation
   (b) Assignment of duties
   (c) Standardisation
   (d) Establishing relationship

8. 'Our assets walk out of the door each evening, we have to make sure they come back the next morning'. This highlights the importance of which function of management:
   (a) Staffing
   (b) Organising
   (c) Planning
   (d) Controlling

9. Which of the following is a financial incentive
   (a) Employee participation
   (b) Promotion
   (c) Job security
   (d) Stock option plan

10. "Hands off" leadership style relates to:
   (a) Participative (b) Autocratic
   (c) Laissez – faire (d) None of the above

11. Labour unions are objecting to the introduction of CCTV (closed circuit television) in a modern tea factory. Which function of management will help in overcoming this issue.
   (a) Staffing (b) Directing
   (c) Controlling (d) Organising

12. 'Kinder Home spaces' started on online business to sell Bed linens, fitted bed sheet sets. They knew that there are other sellers too in their product market. Identify the factors affecting their working Capital Requirements:
   (a) Seasonal factors
   (b) Level of competition
   (c) Production cycle
   (d) Growth prospects

13. Joseph A Schumpeter assigned a crucial role ____________ to entrepreneur.
   (a) Motivation (b) Innovation
   (c) Inventor (d) Organiser

14. Which money market instrument can be issued to individuals, corporations and companies during period of tight liquidity, when deposit growth of bank is slow but demand for credit is high.
   (a) Treasury bill
   (b) Call money
   (c) Commercial bill
   (d) Certificate of deposit

15. Funds which are raised through commercial paper and used for seasonal and working capital needs is known as ____________
   (a) Call Money
   (b) Certificate of deposit
   (c) Bridge financing
   (d) None of above

16. Convincing, luring, attracting customers to buy a product, which marketing philosophy is highlighted here:-
   (a) Selling concept
   (b) Product concept
   (c) Marketing concept
   (d) Production concept

17. Which element of product concept help in fulfilling the Right to information.
   (a) Branding (b) Labelling
   (c) Packaging (d) All of above

18. Informing consumers about their rights and relief available is part of
   (a) Right to safety
   (b) Right to Information
   (c) Right to Consumer Education
   (d) Right to be Heard

19. Name the court where the complain can be filed by the consumer.
(a) District forum
(b) State Commission
(c) National commission
(d) All of above

20. Which Entrepreneurial Competencies is seen in case of Steve Jobs "Apple and I Pod"
(a) Persistence (b) Initiative
(c) Quality performance (d) Motivation

21. Assertion (A): Management principles are not as rigid as principles of pure science.
Reason (R): Human Behaviour is never static and so also technology, which affect business.
(a) Both (A) and (R) are correct
(b) (A) is correct (R) is incorrect
(c) Both (A) and (R) are correct and (R) is the correct explanation of (A)
(d) Both (A) & (R) are correct and (R) is not the correct explanation of (A).

22. Management as on Art has the following features:
(a) Theoretical knowledge and personalised application
(b) Universal Validity
(c) Systematic body of knowledge
(d) None of above

23. A leading company started a school nearby for the children of their employees. Identify the Objective company is fulfilling:
(a) Social objective
(b) Personal objective
(c) Social and personal objective
(d) Organisation objective

24. Name the Fayol's principle of Management which minimizes employee's turnover.
(a) Equity
(b) Fair Remuneration
(c) Stability of tenure of personnel
(d) Sub-ordination of Individual Interest to General Interest.

25. Government attempt to make "Cash lite" economy means:
(a) Channelling more savings through the formal financial stystem.
(b) Improving tax compliance
(c) Both (a) & (b) above
(d) None of the above

26. The retirement age of employee's is 60 years in a company .This is ________ of a company.
(a) Strategy (b) Policy
(c) Rule (d) Procedure

27. Match the terms in Column I with suitable narration in Column II:

	Column-I		Column-II
I.	Delegation	A.	Arises from formal position.
II.	Decentralisation	B.	More control by superiors hence less freedom to take own decision.
III.	Authority	C.	It an optional policy decision. It is done at the discretion of the top management.
IV.	Responsibility	D.	Obligation to perform an assigned task.

Choose the right answer:
(a) I-B, II-D, III-A, IV-C
(b) I-D, II-C, III-B, IV-A
(c) I-B, II-C, III-A, IV-D
(d) I-C, II-D, III-A, IV-B

28. Certain workforce in a factory are unable to learn and understand the working of a new machine. As a result they constantly refer to their supervisor to help them. This leads to lot of wastage of time of the supervisor and also resources of the company.
The Supervisor decided to give them some training. Which one of the following is most suitable in the above case:
(a) On the job training (b) Off the job training
(c) Orientation training (d) Vestibule training

29. Match the Elements of directing in Column-I with their correct meaning in Column-II.

	Column-I		Column-II
A.	Motivation	(1)	The process of watching the employees performing the job.
B.	Communication	(2)	It is activity of influencing people to strive willingly for group objectives.
C.	Supervision	(3)	It is two way process It starts with a sender and ends with a sender.
D.	Leadership	(4)	It is the process which propels people to action and continuous them in action to the best of their ability.

Choose the correct answer:

(a) A (4), B (3), C (1), D (2)

(b) A (1), B (2), C (4), D (3)

(c) A (4), B (2), C (1), D (3)

(d) A (3), B (4), C (1), D (2)

30. Under this style of leadership the leader takes decision in consultation and participation with Employee. This type of leadership style is called:

(a) Democratic (b) Autocratic

(c) Free Run (d) None of above

31. Assertion (A): Controlling function of a Manager is a pervasive function .

Reason (R): Controlling is as much required in an educational institution, Defence Forces, Hospital and a club as in any business organisation .

(a) Both (A) and (R) are true and (R) is the correct explanation of (A)

(b) Both (A) and (R) are true but (R) is not the correct explanation of (A)

(c) (A) is true but (R) is false

(d) (A) is false but (R) is true

32. If there are large number of retired and middle class shareholders who prefer regular income, then a firm should prefer giving ______________

(a) Low dividend (b) High dividend

(c) No dividend (d) Stable dividend

33. If the company wants to raise capital by Debt or Equity, your advise with reason will be:

(a) Debt because ROI > Rate of Interest

(b) Debt because Raising fund as debt is gainful for equity share holder .

(c) Debt because Concept applied here is Trading on equity.

(d) All of above.

34. Risk bearers in a company are:-

(a) Manager (b) Entrepreneur

(c) Intrepreneur (d) Suppliers

35. The existing shareholders are offered right to buy new shares of a company. This is Called:

(a) E - IPOS (b) Rights Issue

(c) Private Placement (d) None of above

36. Rearrange correctly the trading procedure on a stock exchange.

(a) Placing the order

(b) Match the share and best price

(c) Issue of contract Note

(d) Delivery of share and its payment

(e) Opening of Demat account with depository

(f) Execute the order

Choose the correct answer:-

(a) EABFCD (b) DBCEFA

(c) ABECDF (d) AEBCFD

37. Controlling Insider Trading and imposing penalties for such practices comes under the preview of which function of SEBI:-

(a) Development (b) Regulatory

(c) Protective (d) All of above

38. Match the Branding related terms in column-I to its close meaning in column-II:

Column-I		Column-II	
I.	Brand	(1)	That part of brand which is not spoken but identified with sign or symbols
II.	Brand Name	(2)	Any term, name, sign, symbol, design or combination of them to identify the product
III.	Brand Mark	(3)	A brand or part of brand which gives legal, exclusive right to its use
IV.	Trade Mark	(4)	This is verbal component of a brand

Choose the answer:

(a) I (4), II (2), III (1), IV (3)

(b) I (2), II (3), III (1), IV (4)

(c) I (2), II (4), III (1), IV (3)

(d) I (3), II (1), III (2), IV (4)

39. The communication tool which helps in improving the image of the company is

(a) Advertisement (b) Sales promotion

(c) Personal selling (d) Public Relation

40. The consumer protection Act. of 2019 has replaced which act?

(a) The CPA 1982 (b) The CPA 1984

(c) The CPA 1986 (d) The CPA 1988

41. Successful organisation do not achieve their goals by chance but by following a deliberate Process called:

(a) Effectiveness (b) Efficiency

(c) Co-ordination (d) Management

42. A person who keeps Machines, Materials, tools etc. ready for concerned workers, under functional foremanship is called:

(a) Instruction card clerk

(b) Time and cost clerk

(c) Gang Boss

(d) Route clerk

43. A sales person is allowed to close a deal with a buyer giving maximum discount @5% whereas decision regarding any further discount on Puja/ festivals rests with the Sales Manager as the final authority. Identify the principle of Management which is being followed here:-

(a) Centralisation and Decentralisation

(b) Unity of Command

(c) Authority and Responsibility

(d) Unity of Direction.

44. The span of management gives shape to the organisational structure. It means:

(a) It determines the number of departments in a firm.

(b) Number of subordinate that can be effectively managed by a superior

(c) Both (a) & (b) Above

(d) None of the above.

45. Match the sources of recruitment in Column I with their nature of examples in Column II:

Column-I		Column-II	
A.	Web publishing	(i)	Mainly for middle level and top level professional
B.	Management Consultancy	(ii)	www.naukri.com
C.	Campus recruitment	(iii)	Good source of skilled and unskilled operative jobs
D.	Employment exchange	(iv)	Fresh graduates can be moulded as per the requirement of the company

Choose the right answer:

(a) A (i), B (iv), C (iii), D (ii)

(b) A (ii), B (i), C (iv), D (iii)

(c) A (ii), B (iv), C (iii), D (i)

(d) A (iv), B (ii) C (iii), D (i)

46. Assertion (A): Controlling function of a Manager is a pervasive function.

Reason (R): Controlling is as much required in an educational institution, Defence Forces, Hospital and a club as in any business organisation.

(a) Both (A) and (R) are true and (R) is the correct explanation of (A)

(b) Both (A) and (R) are true but (R) is not the correct explanation of (A)

(c) (A) is true but (R) is false

(d) (A) is false but (R) is true

47. A farmer grows organic carrots for the purpose of exports .He has fixed standards for his goods namely Good. Average Reject. Accordingly he has also fixed prices of each bracket. The function followed here is called ________

(a) Grading and Standardisation

(b) Product development and design

(c) Marketing planning

(d) None of above

48. With the help of controlling function, the Management can know not only about the deficiency In the performance but it also helps Management to know whether standards or plans are set correctly or not. The importance of Management discussed above is

(a) Ensuring order and discipline

(b) Judging accuracy of standard

(c) Making efficient use of resources

(d) Facilitating co-ordination in action

49. When target customers are cost conscious and availability in quantity needs to be emphasised which marketing philosophy is used:

(a) Product (b) Production

(c) Selling (d) Marketing

50. Treasury Bills are issued by

(a) Government of India (c) Companies

(b) RBI (d) None of above

SAMPLE QUESTION PAPER 3

Max Marks: 200 Time: 45 min.

General Instruction:

(i) This paper consists of 50 MCQs, attempt 40 out of 50

(ii) Correct answer or most appropriate answer = Five marks (+5)

(iii) Any incorrect option marked will be given minus one marks (–1)

(iv) Unanswer /Marked for review will be given no mark (0)

(v) If more than one option is found to be correct then Five marks (+5) will be awarded to only those who have marked any of the correct option.

(vi) If all options are found to be correct five marks (+5) will be awarded to all those who have attempted the question.

(vii) If none of the options is found correct or a Question is found to be wrong then all candidates who have appeared will be given five marks (+5).

(viii) Calculator/ any electronic gadgets are not permitted.

---

1. Henry Fayol was a
   (a) Social Scientist
   (b) Mining Engineer
   (c) Mechanical Engineer
   (d) Production Engineer

2. Today, the role of global Managers has evolved. They should have:
   (a) Diverse Combination of technical skills
   (b) Soft management and people skills
   (c) The ability to imbibe and learn different cultural experiences
   (d) All of the above

3. Panchayats in our country have been given more powers to decide and spend funds granted to them by the government for welfare of villages. Identify the principles of management highlighted in this statement:
   (a) Authority and Responsibility
   (b) Espirit De Corps
   (c) Equity
   (d) Centralisation and Decentralisation

4. The online and 'work from home' culture globally has helped many firms to remain in market and carry on their tasks. This is related to:
   (a) Political Environment
   (c) Technological environment
   (b) Social environment
   (d) Economic Environment

5. 'Planning is concerned with both ends and means' This statement means
   (a) Setting of objectives and targets of a Company
   (b) Formulating of an action plan for achievement of goals.
   (c) Ends and means are the same thing
   (d) Both (a) and (b) above

6. Planning is closely connected with ____________ and ____________.
   (a) Responsibility and accountability
   (b) Delegation and Decentralisation

(c) Stability and security

(d) Creativity and Innovation

7. Assertion (A): Departmentalisation establishes reporting reletionships.

   Reason (R): It creates hierarchical structure and helps in coordination between different departments.

   (a) Both Assertion A and Reason (R) are true and R is the correct explanation of A.

   (b) Both (A) and (R) are true and R is not the correct explanation of A.

   (c) A is true but R is false

   (d) A is false but R is true

8. The span of management gives shape to the organisation structure. It means:

   (a) It determines the number of departments in a firm.

   (b) Number of subordinates that can be effectively managed by a Supervisor.

   (c) Both (a) and (b) above

   (d) None of above.

9. Analysing existing employees is known as

   (a) Human Resource Management

   (b) Workforce analysis

   (c) Job analysis

   (d) Workload analysis

10. Providing effective directing is a challenging task. Which of these principles do not assist in directing process:

    (a) Harmony of objectives

    (b) Appropriate use of direction

    (c) External Inputs

    (d) Unity of command

11. Controlling is a systematic process involving various steps, which of the following is not a step of in the process of controlling.

    (a) Analysing deviations

    (b) Establishing reporting relationship

    (c) Setting standards

    (d) Taking correcting actions

12. Entrepreneur are related to internal factors, what are they:

    (a) Personality of an individual

    (b) Psychological in nature

    (c) Self Motivation

    (d) all of above

13. Which of this is not a factor affecting the financial decision of a firm:

    (a) Cost of raising fund

    (b) Risk associated with the source of fund

    (c) Control consideration

    (d) Stock market operations

14. Growth opportunities affect dividend decisions because:

    (a) It affects cash flow position

    (b) Firms retain earnings more and declare less dividend

    (c) Dividends are paid out of current and past earnings

    (d) None of the above

15. Assertion (A) "Debt is cheaper but is more risky for a business"

    Reason (R) Payment of Interest and repayment of principal is obligatory for the business

    (a) Both (A) and (R) are true, (R) is the correct explanation of (A)

    (b) Both (A) & (R) are true but (R) is not the correct explanation of (A)

    (c) (A) is true but (R) is false

    (d) (A) is false but (R) is true.

16. Call Money, Commercial paper, Certificate of deposits are instrument of

    (a) Capital Market

    (b) Money Market

    (c) Both (a) and (b) above

    (d) None of above

17. Treasury bills are issued in the form of promissory notes for a minimum amount of ________

    (a) Rs. 2500 (b) Rs. 25000

    (c) Rs. 1000 (d) Rs. 10000

18. Product, price, place and promotion are part of

(a) Product mix (b) Marketing mix

(c) Price mix (d) Place mix

19. The pricing strategy wherein a low initial price is fixed to capture a large market Share is called:

(a) Penetration Pricing

(b) Skim the cream pricing

(b) Both of above (a) & (b)

(d) None of above

20. The Right to Information Act came into force from:

(a) 2004 (b) 1955

(c) 1930 (d) 2002

21. Department of Consumer affairs has been undertaking the campaign through Multimedia awareness namely:

(a) Aap ki Adalat (b) Jago Grahak jago

(c) Upbokta jagran (d) None of above

Read the Text and answer the questions (22-25) below:

Nidhi is a young MBA graduate, Married and joined her husband in Bangalore. She started working as a Manager in a leading food chain company. After the birth of her daughter, she had to quit her job. Looking at the busy schedule of all working women in her areas, she realised there was a need for safe, healthy food outlet. She stumbled upon an idea, which she discussed with her friends & family and decided to Start her own Eatery – Samosa under the brand name of 'Bigg Samosa'. Samosas being a popular Indian snack it was warmly welcomed by people in her locality. She hired two cooks and sold Non-vegetarian and Vegetarian samosas on telephonic order to start with. All home delivered in self created environment friendly packets with their product name printed on the packets. This was a good way to advertise of her venture. 'Nothing beats like word mouth in India'. Her product became very popular in short time and her demand rose many times. She developed whatsapp network connecting prospective customers highlighting her newly added products with their prices. With passage of time her business grew many fold and her products were also available On-line for sale. Orders from school canteen and offices, Kitty & birthday parties were indicating of her success story.

22. Highlight the function of marketing discussed above.

(a) Packaging (b) Market Research

(c) Branding (d) All of above

23. Which elements of promotion mix was used here:

(a) Personal selling (b) Advertising

(c) Both (a) & (b) above(d) None of above

24. The channel of distribution applied by Nidhi was

(a) One level (b) Two level

(c) Zero level (d) None of above

25. Use of WhatsApp and online portal for trading indicate which dimension of business Environment.

(a) Social (b) Technological

(c) Economic (d) Political

26. ________ classified entrepreneur into four types.

(a) Kilby (b) Clarence Danhof

(c) Schumpeter (d) Jeen Baptiste say

27. Assertion (A) Stock Exchange have played a vital role in spreading of Equity cult.

Reason (R) Stock exchanges have taken effective steps in educating the public about investment following better trading practises and regulating new issue.

(a) Both assertion (A) and reason(R) are true and (R) is the correct explanation of (A)

(b) Both (A) and (R) are true and (R) is not the correct explanation of A.

(c) A is true but R is false

(d) A is false but R is true.

28. A note containing the details of number of shares bought/sold, price and other details is called ____________

(a) Depository (b) Credit note

(c) Contract Note (d) Deposit Note

29. SEBI was given a statutory status as a body corporate on

(a) April 1988 (b) Jan 1992
(c) May 1992 (d) July 1994

30. District courts can entertain complaints where value of goods or services does not Exceed________________

(a) 10 crore (b) 1 crore
(c) 5 crore (d) None of above

31. Match the method of Flotation of a company in column I with suitable examples in column II:

	Column-I		Column-II
A.	Prospectus	(i)	First ask the existing share holders to apply for new issue as per the directions under companies Act
B.	E IPO	(ii)	Invitation to public to apply shares through public notice
C.	Private Placement	(iii)	On line system of stock exchange
D.	Right Issue	(iv)	Offer the entire new issue to LIC

Choose the correct answer:

(a) A (i), B (iii), C (ii), D (iv)
(b) A (ii), B (iii), C (iv), D (i)
(c) A (iii), B (ii), C (i), D (iv)
(d) A (i), B (ii), C (iv), D (iii)

32. If the deviations are below the permissible limit in a controlling process, what action Should be taken:

(a) To be reported at top level
(b) Should be ignored
(c) Corrective action to be taken
(d) None of above

33. Raghu joined a government job leaving Private service experience of 8 years. One of the reasons he mentioned was the retirement benefits Government job offered. Which of these highlights retirement benefits:

(a) Medical aid
(b) Dearness Allowance
(c) Pension and Gratuity
(d) Increments

34. The process of converting the message into communication symbols is:

(a) Media (b) Decoding
(c) Feed Back (d) Encoding

35. Match the "Barrier of Communication" in Column I with their examples in Column II:

	Column-I		Column-II
1.	Sematic Barrier	(i)	Status of Superior
2.	Psychological Barrier	(ii)	Lack of proper incentives
3.	Organisational Barrier	(iii)	Faulty translation of Message
4.	Personal Barrier	(iv)	Premature Evaluation

***Choose the answer*:**

(a) 1 (ii), 2 (iii), 3 (iv), 4 (i)
(b) 1 (iii), 2 (iv), 3 (i), 4 (ii)
(c) 1 (iv), 2 (ii), 3 (iii), 4 (i)
(d) 1 (i), 2 (ii), 3 (iv), 4 (iii)

36. Ramesh Kumar a Manager of a firm wants to fix standard of production of a worker In precise quantitative terms. Under which function of Management this can be done:

(a) Controlling (b) Planning
(c) Directing (d) Organising

37. Impact of Demonetisation was noticed in various areas of Indian economy. Which one of the following does not highlight this:

(a) Private wealth (b) Real Estate
(c) Public Sector wealth (d) Digitisation

38. Aiming to revive Jammu & Kashmir's attraction as a top location for film shooting ,the J & K film policy, 2021 offers a host of incentives to the film

makers such as subsidies, long term loans with low interest rates, esp for films with patriotic and certain other themes and for giving work opportunities to local artists etc. This will have an impact on business enterprises in the State, which component of business environment is highlighted above?

(a) Specific &General forces

(b) Economic environment

(c) Technological Environment

(d) Totality of External forces

39. _______ they do not adopt opportunities to make change in production even at a cost of suffering loss:

(a) Innovator (b) Imitation

(c) Fabian (d) Drone

40. Match the following Job with the qualifying tests:

	Column-I		Column-II
A.	Security Officer	1.	Interest Test
B.	Computer Operator	2.	Intelligence Test
C.	A Fashion Designer	3.	Trade Test
D.	College Lecturer	4.	Personality Test

Choose the answer:

(a) A (2), B (3), C (1), D (4)

(b) A (4), B (3), C (1), D (2)

(c) A (4), B (2), C (1), D (3)

(d) A (3), B (2), C (1), D (4)

41. Who are women entrepreneurs? They are firms where

(a) Minimum 51% of the capital owned & controlled by women with minimum 51% women employment.

(b) Minimum 51% of capital owned by women and 100% women employment.

(c) Minimum 100% of capital owned by women and 51% women employment.

(d) None of above.

42. Match the Terms in Column I with most appropriate description in Column II:

	Column-I		Column-II
A.	Importance of organising	(i)	Activities are grouped on the basis of some criteria.
B.	Departmentalisation	(ii)	It leads to occupational specialisation
C.	Advantage of functional structure	(iii)	Conflicts may arise among different divisions.
D.	Disadvantage of Divisional Structure	(iv)	The proper assignment of jobs avoid overlapping of work and better utilisation of resources.

Choose the correct answer:

(a) A (iii) B (iv) C (i) D (ii)

(b) A (iv) B (i) C (ii) D (iii)

(c) A (ii) B (iii) C (iv) D (i)

(d) A (i) B (ii) C (iii) D (iv)

43. Derivative plans are must for accomplishing the objectives of main plan. They are seen in which step of planning process:-

(a) Follow up

(b) Developing premises

(c) Evaluation of different alternatives

(d) Selecting of alternatives

44. Assertion (A) Budget is a statement of expected results expressed in numerical term.

Reason (R) A budget is a controlling devise from which deviation can be taken care of

(a) Both (A) and (R) are not correct

(b) (A) is correct and (R) is incorrect

(c) (A) and (R) are correct and (R) is not the correct explanation of A.

(d) (A) and (R) are correct and (R) is the correct explanation of A.

45. The selection of candidate involves, a series of steps. Arrange them in correct order:

(a) Employment Interview
(b) Job offer
(c) Checking the references
(d) Selection Tests

Choose the correct answer:

(a) D, A, C, B (b) B, D, C, A
(c) C, D, B, A (d) C, B, A, D

46. Pet animals are not allowed in some eatery joints and cafes. This is related to which type of plan:

(a) Strategy (b) Policy
(c) Rule (d) Objective

47. India adopted a policy of Globalisation which means the whole world becomes a global village. The measures taken by the government to adopt this was:

(a) Import Liberalisation
(b) Replacement of FERA to FEMA
(c) Rationalization of Tariff structure
(d) All of the above

48. A private school in a city started extra coaching classes for the students of Class-XII after the official school hours. For this they took extra fees from the students, over and above their regular tuition fee.

For this purpose, some teachers had to stay back after duty hours and give extra hours of teaching. However the school refused to pay them any extra money for extra work. Which principle was violated by them:

(a) Remuneration of employees
(b) Equity
(c) Discipline
(d) Subordination of individual interest to General interest.

49. Assertion (A) Personnel should be selected and appointed after rigorous procedure. Once selected they should be kept in post for a minimum fixed tenure.

Reason (R) Any ad hocism in this regard will create instability among employee.

(a) Both (A) and (R) are correct
(b) A is correct and (R) is incorrect
(c) Both (A) and (R) are correct and (R) is the correct explanation of A.
(d) Both (A) and (R) are correct and (R) is not the correct explanation of A.

50. Functional foremanship is the extension of which principle of management:

(a) Unity of Direction (c) Division of work
(b) Discipline (d) Unity of command

Answers

Sample Paper - 1

1. (d) All of the above
2. (a) Chain of authority and communication
3. (a) Dynamic — ever changing environment and they are all connected.
4. (b) Mental activity. Logical and Systematic thinking for planing is connected to mental activity.
5. (c) Human resource is a non financial parameter.
6. (a) Motivation
7. (d) Organising
8. (a) Wealth maximization
9. (c) Both forward and backward looking function
10. (a) Product
11. (a) Money market
12. (a) Right to be heard
13. (b) Innovation
14. (d) Open Entry — This is not a characteristic of profession.
15. (b) Science not rule of thumb.
16. (a) Liberalisation
17. (b) I - D, II - B, III - A, IV - C
18. (c) Relief to top management
19. (b) Contract of Employment
20. (d) C - E - D - A - B
21. (a) Critical
22. (a) No floatation cost
23. (a) ROI should be higher them rate of interest.
24. (c) Equity trading or Trading on Equity.
25. (a) Both (A) and (R) are correct and (R) is the correct explanation of A.
26. (c) SEBI
27. (c) Both (a) and (b) above
28. (a) Both (A) and (R) are correct and (R) is the correct explanation of A.
29. (d) All of the above
30. (c) Globalization
31. (c) Creativity
32. (c) I - B, II - C, III - A, IV - D
33. (b) (iii), (ii), (i), (iv)
34. (a) I - (iv), II - (i), III - (ii), IV - (iii)
35. (b) Education, Training
36. (c) Employees Recognition Programme
37. (b) Management by Exception
38. (b) ROI = 25%
39. (b) NSDL — National Security Depositary Limited
40. (b) A - (ii), B - (iii), C - (iv), D - (i)
41. (b) Drone Entrepreneur
42. (b) Societal Marketing
43. (c) Labelling
44. (d) All of the above
45. (c) I - 3, II - 4, III - 2, IV - 1
46. (d) All of the above
47. (d) Organisational barrier
48. (b) Authority and Responsibility
49. (c) The person who obtains goods for resale.
50. (b) Electronic Trading System.

Answers

Sample Paper - 2

1. (d) Functions of Management
2. (b) Specialisation. Because many specialist are employed to do those tasks.
3. (a) Contingent
4. (a) Social Environment
5. (c) Technological
6. (c) Planning reduces risk of uncertainty. No one can predict uncertainty.
7. (c) Standardisation
8. (a) Staffing – Human Resources are Assets
9. (d) Stock option
10. (c) Laissez faire
11. (c) controlling
12. (b) Level of competition
13. (b) Innovation
14. (d) Certificate of deposit
15. (c) Bridge Financing
16. (a) Selling concept
17. (b) Labelling
18. (c) Consumer Education
19. (d) All of above
20. (c) Quality performance
21. (d) Both (A) & (B) are correct but (B) is not correct explanation of A.
22. (a) Theoretical knowledge and personalised application.
23. (a) Social objective
24. (c) Stability of tenure of personnel.
25. (c) Channelling more savings through the formal financial system and b) Improving tax compliances.
26. (b) Policy
27. (c) I - B, II - C, III - A, IV - D
28. (a) On the job training
29. (a) A - (4), B - (3), C - (1), D - (2)
30. (a) Democratic
31. (a) Both (A) & (R) are correct and R is the correct meaning of A.
32. (b) High dividend
33. (d) All of above
34. (b) Entrepreneur
35. (b) Right issue
36. (a) E A B F C D
37. (c) Protective
38. (c) I - (2), II - (4), III - (1), IV - (3)
39. (d) Public Relations
40. (d) The CPA 1988
41. (c) Co-ordination
42. (c) Gang boss
43. (a) Centralization and Decentralisation
44. (c) Both (a) & (b) are true
45. (b) A (ii), B (i), C (iv), D (iii)
46. (a) Controlling function required everywhere. Both A and R are true and R is correct explanation of A.
47. (a) Grading and Standarisataion
48. (b) Judging accuracy of standard
49. (b) Production
50. (b) RBI

Answers

Sample Paper - 3

1. (b) Mining Engineer
2. (d) All of the above
3. (d) Principles are Centralisation and Decentralisation
4. (d) Economic Environment
5. (d) Both (a) and (b) above
6. (d) Planning is closely connected with Creativity and Innovation
7. (a) Both A and R are true and R is the correct explanation of A.
8. (b) Span of Management is number of subordinates that can be effectively managed by Supervisor.
9. (c) Job Analysis
10. (c) External Inputs do not assist in directing process.
11. (b) Establishing reporting relationship.
12. (d) All of above i.e. personality, psychological and self motivated person.
13. (d) Stock market operations
14. (b) Firms Retain Earnings more and declare less dividend.
15. (a) Assertion & Reason are true and R is the correct explanation of A.
16. (b) Money Market
17. (b) Treasury bill – Minimum amount of Rs. 25,000.
18. (b) Marketing Mix
19. (a) Penetration pricing – low initial price is fixed.
20. (a) 2004 – Right to Information Act.
21. (b) Jago Grahak Jago.
22. (d) All of above
23. (c) Both (a) & (b).
24. (c) Zero level or B to S direct, no channels.
25. (b) Technology
26. (b) Clarence Danhof classified Entrepreneur of four kinds.
27. (a) A & R are correct & R is correct exp of A
28. (c) Contract Note has details of Name/No. of share bought or sold.
29. (b) Jan 1992 – SEBI got statutory status.
30. (b) 1 crore
31. (b) A (ii), B (iii), C (iv), D (i)
32. (b) Should be ignored
33. (c) Pension and gratuity
34. (d) Encoding
35. (b) Match the following
    1 (iii), 2 (iv), 3 (i), 4 (ii)
36. (a) Controlling
37. (c) Public Sector wealth
38. (b) Economic Environment
39. (d) Drone
40. (b) Match the following
    A - 4, B - 3, C - 1, D - 2
41. (a) 51% of capital owned and controlled by women with 51% of women employees.
42. (b) A (iv), B (i), C (ii), D (iii)
43. (d) Selecting of alternatives
44. (d) A & R are correct
45. (a) D - A - C - B
46. (c) Rule
47. (d) All of above
48. (a) Remuneration of employee
49. (c) Both A & R are correct and R is correct explanation of A.
50. (c) Division of Work.

Points to Crack the CUET (UG)
BUSINESS STUDIES EXAM

As per the announcement given by the Chairman of University Grant Commission, National Testing Agency will be conducting CUET (UG) for undergraduates programmes in Central Universities for every academic session from year 2022 onwards. Many private universities would also like to take admissions on the basis of CUET (UG) scores. This makes CUET (UG) a very important examination.

The first step is to understand the pattern of this examination:

CUET (UG) Includes three section:

Section I: Question based on languages

Section II: 27 Domain based Questions

Section III: General Test

The syllabus is completely based on NCERT – Class XII Business Studies.

The Guidance to crack CUET (UG) in 1st attempt.

- **SWOT Analysis** – Like swot analysis done in a business firm, while preparing for this examination identify your core competency, your strengths i.e. chapters you are confident about. So make your strength areas more strong and focus on your weak areas; identify your threats and take action.
- **Important Terms** – Take out Important terms from each chapter, prepare your notes and the best explanation to the point. This will make your preparation systematic and revision easy. Self learning is the best learning.
- **Years** – Different Legal Acts mentioned with years are important. Make a note of it.
- **Time Test** – Only knowledge of the entire syllabus is not important. To complete the question paper successfully in time is more important. Give yourself practice by taking time tests, solve the sample papers provided after your preparation for exams is over. Complete each sample paper before the allotted time in 45 minutes.
- **Plan your Examination Paper** – all sections of your examination paper should be given time in a judicious manner.
- **Revise the MCQs** – provided in different chapters and your notes to get the desired results.

New Arrival

Books on NTA

CUET (UG)

• *As per latest syllabus* • *Topic-wise MCQs* • *Model Test Papers*

ISBN: 9788178065755 • ₹ **200** • Pg. **96**

ISBN: 9788178065748 • ₹ **260** • Pg. **132**

UNICORN BOOKS

H.O.: F-2/16, Ansari Road, Daryaganj, New Delhi-110002
• **email:** info@unicornbooks.in • **Ph:** 011-23262683, 23250704

Online Presence: Flipkart • Amazon • Meesho